THE
FINANCE
PLAYBOOK
FOR ENTREPRENEURS

Build a solid finance department
for your high-growth business,
without the trial and error

ASIF AHMED

R^ethink

Contents

Introduction

Success in entrepreneurship is a unique concoction of luck, hard work and perseverance – probably in that order. In the game that is roughly 66.6% a function of your decisions, how you execute your job becomes acutely more significant. Think about stacking building blocks: the potential of the whole tower depends on the durability of block one. How it looks, what it's made of, how it's positioned and how well it can sustain bad weather. As the structure grows, so does the dependence on that solitary block. For early-stage businesses, that first block is simply how it structures its finance department. Simple is not the same as easy but in this context refers to habits and processes that look straightforward after they have been explained.

As an entrepreneur, it's wise to recognise that your most valuable lessons will come from getting things wrong. There are no free lunches and frankly no one understands all the problems you are likely to face. As time passes, more and more characters will join your journey and become dependent on your success – whether it's employees, family and friends or simply your own nagging conscience.

You will be doing and learning at the same time, with the pressure and the stakes relentlessly building alongside you. This has been glamourised by the use of the Ray Bradbury imagery of jumping off a cliff and building your wings on the way down. While this is largely true and necessary, some paths such as finance are well trodden. Why waste time figuring it out when the fundamentals are static? Maybe because there don't seem to be any obvious resources. No one has yet rounded up all the best practices and presented them in a digestible format. Gather ten entrepreneurs in the same room and they will have completely different perspectives on business structures, software, taxes and processes. They will always be a result of what they have seen as well as the lessons of the accountant or lawyer they are using at the time.

Everyone has a different opinion because (a) every situation is different and therefore requires a different solution and (b) no one solution will be correct forever and therefore requires constant review. This is why you should never try to copy what your successful friends have done because it probably won't work for you. The only answer is to educate yourself with the basics of technical concepts that never change and arm yourself to ask the right questions for your circumstances. This is a problem that cannot be solved by simply paying for more expensive advisers; they will *simply* charge you more for the wrong answer. I have met countless entrepreneurs who paid eye-watering fees for advice that was fundamentally inappropriate for the business they were trying to create.

I know this because I was an accidental entrepreneur at the age of twenty-three, when my ailing father was no longer able to look after his small accountancy practice. I was a trainee accountant at PricewaterhouseCoopers, completely ill-equipped professionally and mentally to advise other companies, let alone small companies that needed hands-on support. In trying to salvage a deteriorating business as well as support my family, I chose to focus on the only thing I could: processes. Spotting inefficiencies and providing structure around them to make them fall away, I chose to align myself with the nascent start-up community, many of whom were my friends. In 2008 there were very few cost-effective tools available to help with understanding simple things such as book-keeping, software, taxes – all things I could have a large impact on with the benefit of a wide portfolio of companies.

Over the last twelve years, not only has this community grown but so have we as a firm. We have gone on to become leading advisers to high-growth early-stage businesses. My success as an accountant, adviser and leader is bittersweet because I know my father worked hard and chased similar goals to what I have achieved today. Knowing my dad, he would have been working 8am–8pm to this day. At the same time, I wonder how he would have coped with how the world, technology and entrepreneurship have evolved over the last ten to fifteen years. My guess is he would have struggled and held onto his strong foundations as a thoroughbred traditionalist to the point of making himself obsolete. What might that say about some of his contemporaries who continue in practice today?

Setting up your finances, finance department and processes has historically been an operational afterthought, delegated to a numbers person. The teammate who usually prefers a spreadsheet to a normal conversation. Every entrepreneur aspires to get this right but a combination of other priorities results in finance often becoming the problem child of a growing organisation. What ensues is procrastination, heading towards a rude awakening when the company is forced to buckle up via some sort of due diligence process. By then, the founders are likely to have already experienced embarrassment, compromised their chances of successfully completing that transaction and are at short notice compelled to communicate new ways of working across the organisation. No fun and, frankly, no point.

We live in an age where being ahead of the expectation *is* the expectation, although the narrative in the finance world remains so scattered, fragmented and confusing that a company legitimately at the cutting edge of providing algorithmic artificial intelligence solutions is unable to draw up a basic P&L (profit and loss) of its performance. How did that happen?

Clearly the problem doesn't lie in the capabilities of the entrepreneur, as I can assure you that writing code is infinitely more difficult than reconciling bank statements. So then what options does that leave you with as a founder? How can you cut through the noise and take confidence in your finance department living up to the standards of the rest of the organisation? My aim is to help you understand where you have been misadvised, where it was your own fault and what you should do moving forwards.

'Type A' hyper-achieving entrepreneurs use this field of work as a secret weapon. A scaffolding upon which they build their empire, a competitive advantage that quietly serves the entire organisation. But whether they were lucky to have spoken to the right people or simply earned the edge through trial and error doesn't matter – they have what you don't.

For those of you who are blindly wielding your sword on the open battlefield, consider this book a guide on how to build a fortress. A structure worthy of allegiance from bannermen, surrounded by an operational moat to protect against harmful habits, elevated by a watch tower that sees forecastable threats in the distance and a drawbridge to welcome guests, commercial or regulatory alike.

I have played many roles in coming into this knowledge, first as the seeker, then as the observer, but for the last ten years as the designer and teacher. I found myself having the same conversations with ambitious entrepreneurs and the impact of those conversations slowly became a tale of alchemy that to me was second nature. I realised the combination of my unique experiences was what made me particularly well equipped to impart these lessons. I'm an entrepreneur at heart and so I empathise with balancing limited resources with unlimited ambition. I have an unwavering passion for technology and the future of business that keeps me curious about new innovation and efficient ways of solving problems. Most importantly, I am a qualified chartered accountant who has advised hundreds of successful start-ups.

This has a few benefits, which I hope will become apparent as you progress through this book. I understand the accounting, tax and regulatory needs of a business, and because I run my own business, I know what it's like to be an entrepreneur. I have no problem calling out other advisers when they are not right for a certain type of client. Why? Because I do it to myself before I do it to anyone else. How? I know first-hand that the right fit is more important than any fee. I wish more firms felt the same way.

What I am not is a marketeer. It took me some time to realise that the most effective thing I could do for the entrepreneurial ecosystem was to write and share my thoughts with others. It was only after years of conversations with clients and mentees that I realised the basic problems experienced in this field of work by early-stage start-ups tend to be the same – from simple questions such as how to choose an adviser to more nuanced ideas like when to think about raising capital or employing additional people in the finance function.

Maybe on a deeper level I wanted to write the book that might have course-corrected my father's advice had he still been operating as an adviser today. I've wondered what sort of guidance he would have been administering now and what that would mean for the clients we work with today. Would he have advocated for full automation, as someone who spent 90% of his career using ledgers? I'll never know. What I do know is that a lot of his contemporaries – solid, technical accountants – are still practising. Whether it's for him, his clients that never were or just you, today's entrepreneur, this book serves as a blueprint to build your fortress.

You deserve to have access to the tools that can supercharge your company's efficiency and ability to operate as a mature enterprise, even when you're starting out. You will be in the company of successful businesses that you love and admire. At a time when there are only limited outcomes you can control, I urge you to make this one of them.

1

Getting Finance Right – Defining The Problem

It's simple: you've never been taught before. There are no blog posts, no websites and no Twitter storms that could have set you on the right path. It is pretty mind-boggling if you think about it. You might be standing on the frontier of a revolutionary business, with the potential to change the course of history, but there are no tools to help you figure out how to think about finance; culturally, habitually or competitively.

When you're building a business, with everything on the line, the last thing you want to be doing is reading a book about how to manage your receipts. The easiest thing to do is ask a friend, speak to their adviser and carry on with more important work. Totally understandable. This wasn't such a bad strategy over the last fifty years – you could easily rely on a comfortable cocktail of your parents' accountant, the cheapest software and a baseline level of knowledge that would tide you over until it didn't have to be your problem anymore. Anecdotal evidence suggests that budding entrepreneurs are much more likely to use the family accountant to help them with their new venture than seek an alternative. That makes intuitive sense, and it works like this with lawyers, too (though it often helps that they know a bit about your family). It definitely works this way with doctors. Why wouldn't the same apply to accountants? This inaugural decision sets you up for a career of treating finance and accounting as a passive afterthought.

What follows is a series of similarly passive decisions in the early stages of your business at a time when you are laying the foundations for everything that follows. It infiltrates how you think about processes, how rigorously you scrutinise detail and how urgently you wise up to your need to gain knowledge. Sound like you?

Maybe you're the kind of founder who is really on top of the detail, with Excel workbooks that put every coffee receipt you have ever received into a pivot table. The problem is that neither you nor your parents' accountant knows for sure whether what you are doing is going to help you get where you are headed – surely that's more important than knowing exactly which branch of Starbucks that receipt came from?

I speak of receipt management facetiously, but it is not a trivial matter. It is so untrivial a matter that I could personally tell you of at least four stories of successful businesses that went bust because of how bad their system of collating receipts was. By the end of this book, you should appreciate that cultivating excellence in the detail leads to the greatest results. Taking the opposite approach leaves you with, well, a good reason to speak to one of those four ex-CEOs.

Why are expectations different now?

While it might be true that no two entrepreneurs are on the same path, there are certainly some universal truths that apply to all of us seeking to operate effectively. The goal posts have not only moved, they are constantly moving, more frequently than ever before. The entrepreneurial game is now about seeking out the inches. Technologies such as Amazon Web Services and the Google Suite have levelled the playing field, resulting in lower barriers to entry, new business models emerging and every enterprise having the capability to be instantly global. The operational inches are often where battles are won or lost, a phenomenon that those that came before us did not experience as acutely.

In fact, the evolution has been so exponential that many seasoned advisers now find themselves short of relevant advice as so much of their accepted wisdom has been superseded. This doesn't stop them from giving that advice. It is amazing how much damage an experienced, well-meaning, well-regarded adviser can do when faced with a business that is charting a path or industry they have never seen before. In some cases, arguably more damage than you could have inflicted without any advice. It's not your fault – how were you to know?

CASE STUDY: THE TECH CEO

In 2017, our firm was introduced to Melissa, a twenty-five-year-old CEO who was building a deep-tech business and needed new advisers as her parents' accountant had sadly passed away. At our first meeting she took out two ring-binders, which she aptly described as her 'books'. In this folder were pages and pages of handwritten records of monies in and out with a replicated spreadsheet that she had maintained to 'make the calculations easier'.

Upon my asking, she recalled that when her father introduced her to the family accountant, his exact words were, 'I don't understand all this artificial intelligence stuff, but buy yourself a sales day book and cash ledger and fill it in every day and bring it to us at the end of the year.'

While my colleagues and I sat stunned by the irony of a computer science graduate maintaining handwritten records, she proceeded to vent that there must be a better way of doing this and, if there wasn't, how much would it cost to outsource this graft to us?

Within five minutes of opening her eyes to a world of automation and process-driven compliance, she was speechless. The kind of silence that can only be rooted in introspection, an ode to all the time she had wasted and a reminder that sometimes it really is the blind leading the blind.

When the global economy is driven by technology and data, the only lessons that hold true from the past are the 'first principles'. Those old adages probably make your teeth itch – how relevant is 'cash is king' to an entrepreneur who is losing cash for fun every month? Turns out, pretty damn relevant.

You probably already knew that, but nobody ever tells you where to go from there. In charting triumphs of history against accepted wisdom for today, we are in what I call the sticky middle. Instructions are conflicting, information is asymmetrical, some stumble upon best practices but most travel blind, nursing one wound and then the next. The leaders of the finance and accounting world did not build their careers with modern practices as the norm. The modern entrepreneur is left with no choice but to assimilate the best war stories passed down through the ages, speak to family and friends about what they did when they were in business and hope it will work for them too.

They become an amalgamation of all the people, habits (often bad) and processes they have encountered on their journey with only hindsight to know if it was the right strategy or not. Sound like you? If so, I think you'll like this book.

Fewer wants, more needs

There is no 'one size fits all' framework but there are what we might call 'new first principles' that history has not had a chance to condense into easily digestible proverbs. Those who nail them have an advantage over competition to the point where it becomes a competitive advantage. A bit like when 'cash is king' was something only a few understood, until the point it became common knowledge and then a meme.

It stands to reason that you must seek a basic education in the subject and the tools to make the right decisions at every stage of your journey. However, no transformation can take place until you have a clear vision of what you want from your finance function versus what you need. Start with the latter – treat it like baseline health. There really is no point walking over pounds to collect pennies. This will be a consistent theme in the forthcoming chapters. Once you have consensus over what you need, you can take a moment to recognise that you have already entered the paradigm of supercharging your entire business. What will follow is a raft of 'wants' that will be naturally occurring by-products of an uncompromising foundation of core abilities and processes.

How you think about your finance function – its processes, role and importance – often becomes the definition of how you are regarded as an entrepreneur.

It speaks to discipline, resource allocation and pri-
oritisation of fundamentals, traits that will stand any
leader in good stead, particularly one who is charting
unknown territory. It is a business within a business
and the only function that plays attack, defence, goal-
keeper and manager at the same time. If you are not
reliant on, at the mercy of and, frankly, slightly scared
of your finance function, you have this all wrong.

Underpinning this strategy is the desire to reframe
the narrative around finances and shift the focus from
understanding the past towards informing the future.
The difference between these two stances defines
whether your finance function is an administrative or
strategic function of the business. This book will only
ever make the case for the latter and provide the tools
to ensure that is the case.

Talk about how you do things

Treating the finance function as a competitive advantage is a weapon that only the best entrepreneurs
recognise. Whether in conversation with new staff
members, customers or investors it is almost impossible not to delve into the inner workings of your
processes, intentionally or unintentionally. This is
why it is advisable that entrepreneurs volunteer an
insight into their resilient, best-in-class infrastructure
that fuels all the amazing things the wider business is
doing. It is reassuring for an incoming staff member to

THE FINANCE PLAYBOOK FOR ENTREPRENEURS

know there is a reference document of all of the company's financial procedures for them to read on their first day. It is comforting to a customer to know that your invoicing is accurate and automated. No one is more impressed than an investor for whom you are able to generate intricate and incisive company performance records at a minute's notice. While this might sound like a great aspiration, recognise it is par for the course.

For early-stage businesses, it may not be possible or necessary to achieve this immediately, but you should strive for it from the start – a mindset and dedication that can either be embraced proactively or deferred perilously. The prolific value investor Warren Buffett said, 'You only have to do a very few things right in your life so long as you don't do too many things wrong.'[1] This book aims to equip you with the very few 'right things'.

It struck me that if I was going to say there is currently no singular framework that works for everyone, surely it was worth noting the few things that do. This will be the basic education upon which you must build, using the principles that unfold. Today's entrepreneur must be deliberate, thoughtful, intentional, proactive rather than reactive and sit at the heart of what we will refer to as the 'finance fortress'. This will be the

1   B Snyder, '7 insights from legendary investor Warren Buffet', *make it*, CNBC (1 May 2017), www.cnbc.com/2017/05/01/7-insights-from-legendary-investor-warren-buffett.html, accessed 27 June 2021

sum of all the learnings we pick up over the course of this book and will serve as a blueprint.

This is a living, breathing organism that operates the anatomy of your entire business but, rather than a specific organ, consider this your central nervous system.

Summary

- It is not your fault if you are bewildered with finance, but that doesn't change the fact it is your job to get it right.

- Finance, tax and accounting knowledge is disparate and difficult to piece together; goal posts are consistently moving. It's a game of inches – you have no choice but to wise up to what matters, quickly.

- You can start with first principles but be aware that textbooks were not written for your business – you must apply your business to the textbooks.

- Your finance function must be part of your competitive advantage as a business.

- Design and build your finance fortress as early as you can. It will serve to protect, inform and fortify.

2

What Sort Of Business Are You? The Specifics

Walk with me through the hallways of this large co-working office block. There are hundreds of companies. Some with rows and rows of staff members with headsets on, with three or four screens each, and others with just two people working quietly as if they don't recognise one another in the same room.

We walk into the breakout area and there is a dynamic atmosphere of people having meetings, relaxing, or on the phone. As you look around there are endless layers of commonalities as well as distinguishing features between these entrepreneurs, but you and I both know they are all here to work. How is it possible they can all be engaging in the same activity yet at this snapshot in time be cutting such wildly different figures?

For every entrepreneur, there is a slightly different business model at work and what you are witnessing is modern business playing out in real time. It turns out that the two people we walked past earlier are in fact the co-founders of an online business on which they started using their own savings only a couple of years ago. Over the last two years, they have revenues in excess of £2 million. They have no external shareholders, and all of their production and stock is managed and delivered from a central factory and warehouse. They are assisted by a team of four remote staff members who work across two time zones and the only physical office space the company maintains is the one we walked past.

On the other hand, another young woman on the phone is the CFO (chief financial officer) and co-founder of a venture-backed technology business looking to raise her next round of funding. They have half a dozen full time software engineers and the same again in sales and business development. If their last valuation was anything to go by, they are working towards building a business that could exit (sell) in five years' time for anywhere between £50 million and £75 million but, as of today, they have three months' cash left in the bank, hence the phone call.

Having a firm grip on what kind of business you are going to be should dictate every decision you make in the early days. Undertaking this introspective exercise helps cultivate urgency where it is needed and alleviates pressure where it isn't. There is so much to think about, and it helps to know what path is relevant to you, whether it's matters of technology or how detailed your key performance indicators (KPIs) need to be. While I may have conveniently taken you for a walk through the only co-working space in which I personally know two companies on the same floor, it stands to reason that doing this analysis requires some sort of decision tree. Once you have decided which category you fall under, you must stay firm on all of the expectations and merits of that path. The path is the gift.

The table below breaks down the various types of business.

Lifestyle businesses

A lifestyle business is often looked down on as a hobby that generates a bit of cash, nothing too serious or strenuous. While this might be true for many, some seriously successful businesses also fall under the same category. With little operational overhead and infrastructure, simple demand and supply can mean a well-designed lifestyle business can generate enviable profit and cashflow.

Category	Definition	Stakeholders	Finance processes
Lifestyle	Niche product or service managed by five or fewer people with the express intention to remain this way	The owner-managers Customers Staff Regulatory bodies	Compliance Basic KPI management Assisted by technology
Growth (owner managed)	Wide appeal product or service with strong ambitions to grow exponentially	The owner managers Customers Staff Regulatory bodies Target stakeholders, eg new customers, potential investors, potential acquirers	Compliance Mature KPI management in line with growth plans Guided by technology
Growth (external investors)	Wide appeal product or service with a commitment to grow exponentially as a moral and fiduciary duty to their supporters	Shareholders Customers Staff Regulatory bodies Target stakeholders	Compliance Mature KPI management in line with committed plans Reliant on technology

What differentiates one from the other? By definition, lifestyle businesses are primarily designed around the life the founder wishes to have. Whether it's running your business Monday to Thursday from your spare room with a three-day weekend or from a vegan café in Bali, the choice is yours. It stands to reason that with a good internet connection and laptop most people can sell products and services that don't require physical interaction with the end customer.

Sounds pretty idyllic, but a successful lifestyle founder recognises that the ideal lifestyle is a by-product of relentless reliance on strong processes and discipline, with the aim being to keep the lifestyle going. Teams are substituted for distributed workflows and physical assets are replaced with intellectual assets. At the same time, the absence of being physically available some of the time normally means having to be virtually available all of the time.

Growth (owner managed)

This is the kind of business that we all typically associate with the term small-medium enterprise (SME), be it a married couple looking to start a business together or two colleagues breaking away from their employer to found a new start-up of their own. The express desire is to build out a hypothesis that could later turn into something much larger. These businesses are always at risk of the 'sticky middle' syndrome.

Without clear definition of what the business intends to be, it is difficult to know whether to build for lifestyle or for something greater. This often leaves these businesses rudderless, without adequate processes and discipline. While the need to be compliant is no different, the wider company must operate in accordance with where it is heading.

Without that being clearly defined, the inner workings of these companies tend to reflect that level of confusion.

Growth (external investors)

When a company requires more capital than it is initially able to generate itself, it will seek support from outside investors. Initially this may be friends and family but as the business grows it will seek more substantial sums from professional investors (angels, venture capitalists or even private equity). These circumstances bring an added layer of what are known as 'fiduciary duties', ie an obligation to act in the best interest of another party. If people have entrusted you with their money to build out your hopes and aspirations, you owe them a duty of service to build that company in a responsible way. Alongside your compliance obligations (filing accurate accounts and taxes) you are compelled to implement robust processes, frameworks and systems that deliver on those responsibilities. You will need to report back to your investors with meaningful information born out of reliable data that is a function of a watertight finance protocol that permeates your entire organisation.

There are nuances to all of the above but thinking about your company through this lens helps set you up for the journey you are about to embark upon. It is also true that within each of the above there are layers that mean no two companies will have exactly the same requirements. For example, if you are planning on setting up a boutique online bakery that showcases your talents to your local area, you might be doing this purely for the love of your craft. However, as the moving parts of your business are reasonably easy to stay on top of, you are unlikely to require as sophisticated an infrastructure as the pet food retailer with the £2 million revenue, even though both would be considered lifestyle businesses.

These layers are evident in high-growth companies funded by external investors. This is normally because the introduction of external capital propels the company onto a journey that the founding team may not have experienced before. This is particularly the case with first-time founders who have not operated companies or managed large sums of institutional capital. This is a daunting enough prospect as it is without the pressure of having to navigate through the conflicting messages. Which advisers should we work with? How do we hire the right staff? What processes should be implemented? What documentation should the company maintain? What metrics should be measured?

People need most assistance when building companies that are looking to traverse through each of the above forms, ie start as a lifestyle business, see how that goes then maybe look to expand if the opportunity arises, possibly raising external capital if the growth plan demands it. These companies will go through many iterations and often there will be a conflict between wanting to keep things simple and keeping the door open to future opportunities.

At the start of any business adventure, the founding team should have an honest discussion about exactly what type of business you are looking to build. Write it down. Everything from this point onwards – culture, attitudes, budgets and processes – will be driven by this foundational assertion. Not doing this is the equivalent of setting off from Luton Airport in your twin-engine light aircraft for a leisurely trip, only to decide part way through your journey that you'd like to carry on to Sydney. It won't happen – and on the slim chance it does, not only are you lucky, but you've also probably spent a lot more of your investors' money than you needed to but critically lost time you are not going to get back.

Using the categories identified above, this conversation can be a good way to tease out misalignment and bridge any expectation gap where there might not have obviously been one. Once a consensus is achieved, it provides the perfect jumping off point to set up the 'table stakes' for that category of business.

Summary

- Critically align your business with a specific growth path and commit to the responsibilities that path demands. It is better to head in one direction consciously than many directions carelessly.

- The path is the gift.

- It is likely your company will span different categories across different phases of your existence. Don't use this as an excuse to hold off on implementing mature processes as early as possible – it will only benefit your business in the long run.

- Ensure your management team are on board with this direction and the individual responsibilities they must assume as a result. If they are not right for the journey, they are not right for this role.

- Introducing external stakeholders such as shareholders brings additional responsibilities; this is no longer your business. Your systems must reflect this and no number of other priorities will erase that fact.

3
Advisers – How To Choose The Right One

When I talk about advisers, I really mean accountants. You know you need them, but you're not equipped to know how to choose one, and there are thousands. When starting out, it is likely that a firm of accountants (or lawyers) are the first external advisers you encounter, possibly to help set up your company. Your requirements will be limited. You are typically driven by your budget – understandable as all you need is someone to assist with the basics (company formation, annual filings, ad hoc advice). I have spent my entire career in this field, starting off at the largest accountancy firm in the world and going on to build two successful firms thereafter. I have seen all sorts of businesses become clients and through that process learned some valuable lessons about which adviser/client relationships work and which don't. The nature of your relationship with your accountant can be the defining factor in early-stage success.

Framing the dilemma

The earliest challenge for new entrepreneurs is the pressure of having to make foundational choices about the structure of their business at a point when they have the least knowledge, experience and budget. Deciding on which adviser or firm of advisers to work with should be treated exactly like any other long-term commitment. A bad choice of adviser not only leads to bad decisions for the company, but a series of more problematic consequences also play out, including:

- The founder never being equipped nor encouraged to ask the right questions of an accountant

- Blindly accepting recommendations and advice without the ability to corroborate or understand whether it sounds right for their circumstances

- Commercially advancing in their career without commensurately upskilling their knowledge of fundamental accountancy, finance, and taxation concepts, which leads to a long-term blind spot and dependency on others to make key decisions

The quality of a relationship can only be assessed in hindsight, after a lot of time and money has been spent. The chances are the relationship was forged through an introduction and recommendation by a trusted source and so, at the start, there is no real reason to think it won't be a success. Thus emerges a blameless paradox that both entrepreneurs and accountants find themselves in. A handful of those relationships go on to be productive long-term client-adviser relationships but many more end up becoming transactional and hollow.

How on earth is a new entrepreneur supposed to know how to navigate this problem? Is it even their problem to navigate? The answer to that second question is simple: yes. You will find this to be a key theme of this book: 'The chips are stacked against you but if you want to win, stop whining, do X and move on.'

One significant failure of the accountancy profession is the absence of an engagement refusal culture. If this concept was more prevalent, a natural order would prevail between different business types with suitable advisers.

I believe my greatest strength is being honest when we are not going to be suitable for a given client. Below is an example of how this is managed:

Dear Joe

Thank you for giving us the opportunity to work with XXXX Ltd.

Unfortunately, I do not think we are going to be able to assist you with the journey you are about to embark upon. As a Fintech business you are going to need to make quarterly filings to the Financial Conduct Authority (FCA), which we do not have the expertise to assist with. We can assist by:

1. *Introducing you to a regulatory consultancy that would charge additional fees to ours to assist with this – if budget permits.*

2. *Introducing you to another firm of accountants with in-house expertise on the specific regulatory requirements as well as the scope you have asked us to assist with.*

3. *Sending you a proposal only for the areas we are experts in and help you identify a person to hire in-house as part of your finance team to help with the remainder.*

Look forward to speaking with you.

Asif

When we do commit to working with a new entrepreneur, we lead with an offer to educate as well as advise. This means we are inherently unable to work with a large volume of clients, though this isn't the business model of many small practices. While some may operate with the same transparency, the sheer number of individual practitioners in the market means that entrepreneurs are likely to meet a whole raft of personalities and organisations without having an adequate toolkit by which to make a critical decision. Another negative result of there being so many small firms is that the odds of finding the right fit are now squarely against the entrepreneur.

Changes in the accounting industry

When my father set up his accountancy practice in the early 1980s, he and his contemporaries were regarded as the conduit to almost every element of their clients' businesses. I remember going to his office, where there would always be one or two people in the reception waiting to see him. After giving him a quick wave, I would make my way to the back room to see my mother (his secretary), who would be on the phone at her desk, nestled between five filing cabinets. The client in reception could have been anyone ranging from Mr Murphy – managing director of a local construction business who had come to find out his Value Added Tax (VAT) liability – to Mrs Wong, who had one rental property but was always perpetually nervous about her tax bill, up to seven months before the deadline.

The office felt pivotal, not only to our livelihood as a family but to tens of other families who treated those meetings as significant to their everyday lives. You may read this and reminisce about similar experiences you had in that era, not only with your accountants but with the bank manager and other important strategic relationships. Many more of you will remember them as a monumental waste of time against the backdrop of how far technology has come since then. Herein lies the problem.

Many small firms are now struggling to keep up with being able to charge for services that have been completely overtaken by software and advice that is now freely available on the internet. The natural remedy to this is for these firms to take one of two possible strategies:

1. Take on even more clients to soften the impact of reduced revenues. The upshot is diluted focus, attention and knowledge of individual client circumstances, an emphasis on commoditising services, and a generalisation of advice.

2. Take the harder route – embrace technology, upskill and focus on more profitable value-added services for a smaller pool of clients.

Historically, a large revenue stream was collating bags of receipts and entering them into a spreadsheet. Sounds backwards now, but for the average managing director of a local construction business the fear of Her Majesty's Revenue & Customs (HMRC) turning up at your doorstep far outweighed any desire to learn Microsoft Excel and save on fees.

While firms are slowly moving away from these manual processes, some are still out there and might be the ones you end up meeting in the early days of your business, whether due to the relationship your parents have had with them for the last thirty years or because you are not equipped to know where else to look. As the computer scientist and entrepreneur Paul Graham says, 'When experts are wrong, it's often because they're experts on an earlier version of the world.'[2]

The services you need from your accountants

The level of knowledge a given entrepreneur has at the point of engaging an accountancy firm varies from person to person. Sometimes the client isn't 100% sure what services are required from the relationship. Most founders know that there is a basic level of compliance required but the details around which exact services, when they are relevant and how much they should cost is always confusing.

I have summarised these services into categories to make it easy to understand the difference between housekeeping services and value-added services.

---

2   Paul Graham, 'How to be an expert in a changing world' (December 2014), www.paulgraham.com/ecw.html, accessed 23 June 2021

Housekeeping

Personal tax/self-assessment: Every director of a limited company must complete a self-assessment tax return every year by the end of January (for online submissions) and the end of October (for paper returns) for the preceding tax year (6 April–5 April).

Company accounts: Every limited company must file iXBRL (inline eXtensible Business Reporting Language) compatible accounts to Companies House and HMRC every year.

Company corporation tax: Along with your accounts, you are also required to file a corporation tax return to HMRC every year, declaring your profits and tax thereon.

VAT returns: Companies registered for VAT must file (typically) quarterly returns to HMRC to declare the net VAT collected or refundable to the business.

Payroll: If you employ staff, you will need to process your payslips on a weekly/monthly basis, as well as calculate the PAYE (pay as you earn) and employer tax liabilities for each period.

Company secretarial services: This is the process by which you maintain your official company register, eg register of directors and register of members, and ensure the public information about the company is up to date with Companies House.

Value-added services

Management accounting: These are the figures management use to make business decisions, ie period P&L, cashflow statements and important KPIs.

Government grants: Companies pursuing innovation in the field of science and/or technology may be eligible for government subsidies or grants, eg research and development tax credits or direct funding for projects through bodies such as Innovate UK.

Tax-efficient fundraising: (Seed Enterprise Investment Scheme, Enterprise Investment Scheme). If you are looking to raise capital from private investors, qualifying for any of the above schemes can make your business a tax efficient investment proposition. Naturally, navigating the requirements and assisting with the administration is a service often provided by accountancy firms.

Board advisory services: As a young business, it is likely that you are aware of the statutory requirements and documentation required to be executed and maintained by a Board of Directors.

Employee share option schemes: When looking to implement a long-term incentive plan for staff members, involving equity participation, you are likely to require an HMRC approved share option scheme. As the requirements and documentation are complex an accountancy firm will often be best placed to assist with the implementation.

Regulatory filings: Depending on the nature of your business, it is possible that you are obliged to make additional filings to an industry or trade body/ regulator such as the FCA or Air Travel Organiser's Licensing. These filings are often best made by industry specialists, but some accountancy firms may have a sub-specialism in these areas.

Specialist services

Corporate finance: Unlikely to be an early-stage requirement but deals with how businesses think about capital structure, ie debt and equity and investment decisions, accordingly.

Mergers and acquisitions advisory: Due diligence services where a business may be considering acquiring another company or possibly getting acquired themselves.

The different types of firm

Historically, there has been no attempt to categorise accountancy firms beyond the Top Four, Top Ten, or

Top Fifty. This loose list of roughly the same names appearing year on year ranks firms by revenue. How this is relevant or useful information is anybody's guess but as a reader it doesn't equip you with anything other than knowing that PricewaterhouseCoopers, Deloitte, KPMG and Ernst & Young form the Big Four, and have since time began. The chances are you won't be working with them, at least not yet, so how do you decide who to work with today?

There are so many names and outwardly they all look the same. Your friends will have worked with some, your parents will have worked with others but here you are, having to decide what's best for you with no guidance. It is hard to wade through the long tail of medium and small firms. You begin to appreciate how, rightly or wrongly, firms that are familiar, local or 'in the family' end up being the first port of call for any new entrepreneur.

Professional services are fundamentally a relationship-based business and relationships transcend brands. While this fact doesn't help you with your decision making, it should help cement the notion that finding the right provider for you and your business has nothing to do with the brand name and everything to do with the person you're working with. In this book, I will attempt to condense this disparate profession into easily digestible concepts. While many will argue that the categories are clumsy and broad, my aim is to help you, not them. I prefer not to refer to small- and medium-sized firms because it is almost impossible to define which is which. You will know them when you see them. These are the three main categories:

1. Generalist firms

- Typically, fewer than three principals
- Work with many small businesses and are industry agnostic
- Offer basic compliance work as main service
- Charge a fixed fee

2. Specialist firms

- Work with a specific industry or type of client
- Have deep domain expertise
- Offer basic compliance work but have multiple value-added services to assist with growth
- Combination of fixed and variable fees

3. Large firms

- Mentioned specifically as their brand reputation is often more valuable than their expertise; in most cases, if you choose to work with them, it is because both elements are equally important to you (eg for optical reasons in front of investors, public markets, etc)

- Multiple areas of deep domain expertise
- Do not offer compliance work
- Typically, all fees are variable, ie timesheet by the hour

This is by no means a hierarchy nor an indication of better or worse. It is simply a condensing of my experiences, having worked with hundreds of companies and having worked in and for each category of firm. You make your own decisions about which firm falls into which category through your interactions with them. In your mind, it is important to label each option you might be considering accordingly and assess their suitability against the flowchart and your needs.

Science vs beauty contest

If you have clearly chalked out the path your business is going to take, you will need to distil the support, skills and expertise required for that journey. Work with the adviser who is equipped to assist you for where you are going, not where you are.

While we are unearthing the structural flaws of small firms, it is important to mention that the same problem exists with the 'trophy' firms. I used to work for one of them. The consequences of a bad 'fit' exist regardless of the size of the firm – do not assume bigger is *always* better. Choosing the right firm to work with is an undocumented science rooted in logic, much like making an appointment with the right kind of doctor. You wouldn't go to a general practitioner if you wanted to achieve optimum heart health – a cardiologist would be far better suited.

Below is a simple matrix through which to view the decision-making process when courting a raft of varying options or recommendations.

	Housekeeping	Value-added service	Specialist services
Lifestyle	A	B	B
High-growth – exit > three years	B	B	B
High-growth – exit < three years	B	C	C

While this may be a handy guide to reinforce the point that start-ups need to work with specialist firms, the matrix becomes even handier when analysed with the following additional perspectives:

- How well does your team understand finance, accounting and tax? If the answer to that is 'really well', then working with a category A firm will likely prove an economical and reasonable decision. However, if the answer is anywhere between 'OK' to 'not at all', working with a general practice is unlikely to assist your personal growth and making the investment in a category B firm will likely be well worth it.

- Where do you see your business in five years' time? While on the surface this is a vague question, it forces you to wrestle with whether the firm you are sitting in front of today will fit the bill for where you are aiming to be in five years. Does this practice already operate, with other clients, where you see yourself being?

- Is it possible for you to use different providers for different services?

It's not always that simple. You are likely to start off with a category A firm with the full intention of progressing through to a B and eventually a C. That is not to say that A to C is an aspirational path, it may just be the path you choose to take.

The firm you decide to work with in the early stages of your business automatically speaks to your personal growth path as an entrepreneur and the foundations your business will lay down, as well as the importance you place on goals.

Whether you are time poor or just not minded in this field, the success of a client-adviser relationship is always a two-way dynamic. You are investing in your future, not delegating your current workload. Work with a firm that will educate you to achieve your goals. This relationship should be an education for you as an operator. If over time the quality of your questions is not improving, you are not in the right relationship.

The only way to know whether this will be possible is through developing your own screening process when approaching a potential suitor. Here are some example questions to ask:

1. How will you assist me in setting up adequate processes within my business to maximise efficiency?

2. Please provide a reference from another business you wouldn't mind me contacting to understand the nature of the relationship we are likely to have.

3. Please provide a list of suitable tasks we can retain in-house to ensure we are bettering our own understanding of compliance.

4. Please provide three separate scales of fees, citing your services and exclusions in each case.

5. Please provide a list of pertinent issues (from your domain) that you believe we face as a business of this size in [industry].

6. What specific services do you believe we are likely to need that you are unable to provide?

7. Which firms do you have direct relationships with to assist us with Question 6?

You are trying to understand whether you are a good fit for each other and, critically, for how long. The elephant in the room is the key topic of fees. Questions 3 and 4 will help to reach an arrangement where you can begin a working relationship with each other regardless of your current circumstances. However, it stands to reason for all of the structural issues I mentioned earlier that fees are often the main competing ground for firms to win new business.

This is a negotiation strategy skewed heavily in the firm's favour rather than yours as a company. While they may ultimately economically benefit from your engagement, you run the risk of making an ineffective decision for your business if the strategic fit isn't right. Work with the right firm at the right fee rather than the wrong firm at a discounted fee.

A further variable to this decision is the ability to retain a relationship with more than one firm at any given time. You may have a fruitful relationship with a given organisation but deep down know there are specialist services you will need, eg corporate finance, that your day-to-day advisers simply do not have the capability to assist you with. The answers you receive to Questions 6 and 7 will help establish whether your firm is able to play a gatekeeping role for you into the future, with the ability to leverage your long-standing relationship to ensure you end up in safe hands.

Empathy is key

Being an entrepreneur is a gruelling and often lonely pursuit. As matters progress, the number of confidantes you can have open conversations with becomes smaller and smaller. I have the great privilege of being one of those people to many successful entrepreneurs and I like to think *that* side of the business relationship is as important as any. The greatest trait your adviser should have is empathy.

The ability to communicate with you as an equal as well as an adviser is a rare trait that transcends any fancy business card and should be the overarching non-negotiable. This is where references are essential and regular communication in the early days is a suitable test ground to form a rapport.

Similarly, it is critical that your chosen firm is able to guide you on both a macro and a micro level. They should have broad understanding of your industry with deep knowledge of their domain within it. It is too often the case that the trade-off between a technically minded versus commercially minded accountant is skewed towards the former. This can begin to affect your attitude towards this field of work too. You want to ensure that the decisions you are making today are finessed with the sum total of the experience your adviser has amassed over the years of working with other entrepreneurs. This is where the value in the fees lies, not in the ability to file things on time.

Your development as an operator and business owner should be the standout by-product from this relationship; it is important to look for early signs that this will be the case.

In building the finance fortress, your accountant should be the chief engineer who helps understand the requirements of the structure both now and in the future, providing a design that is equipped for that journey. As time progresses and the nature of the battles shift, they continue to be well placed to know the modifications required and draw on past examples of comparable fortresses that weathered similar adversaries. Most importantly, the chief engineer continually educates the chief executive or chief of finance to make structural decisions of their own, using the values laid within the foundations.

Summary

- Work with the adviser who is equipped to assist you for where you are going, not where you are.

- Work with the right firm at the right fee rather than the wrong firm at a discounted fee. Fit is more important than fees. Always negotiate the latter to match the former.

- Always apply a screening process with every new adviser, testing them on matters you are due to face now, next year and in five years' time.

- Invest in an adviser who will help you grow as a business operator. You must consistently feel that you are learning from them.

- Be comfortable in using different advisers for different roles – that may be category A for some things and category C for others.

- If you sense a lack of empathy in their demeanour, it should be an unreserved deal-breaker.

- Pay for value and economise on processes and have the ability to decipher between the two.

4

Growing Up – Professionalise Your Finance Department

Growing up is not the same as growing old. The latter happens passively while the former is an active decision that companies are either wise to or deflect at their peril. In the school of entrepreneurship, there are no defined grades or exams for you to know when you have 'graduated' from one class to the next – it is a personal pursuit that entrepreneurs and their teams can take as early or as late as possible. This is maybe the highest price entrepreneurs pay for taking themselves out of the 'intellectual conveyer belt' that a steady corporate job provides. All learning, upskilling and maturity is now squarely a function of your own initiative. As a result, so is the art of providing feedback, setting goals and being direct with recognising weaknesses. There is an enormous difference between being a genuine entrepreneur and someone who is simply looking for less accountability by being their own boss.

In the field of finance, processes and governance there are no rewards for youth, youthful thinking or under-cooked knowledge. However, the proactive decision to 'grow up' and get with the need of the hour applies as much to first-time founders as it does to repeat founders who may be facing a new set of challenges. Complacency and a sense of entitlement rarely bear fruit. Whether you are an entrepreneur wanting to future-proof your company or an established busi-ness standing at the foot of a transformational growth plan, it is in your interests to go through a 'growing up health check'.

Growing up means stepping back and critically assessing each element of your finance structure, doc-umentation, team and systems and ensuring they are optimised for the journey you are embarking on while also reflecting on whether you are the right person to be making that assessment.

Structure

Deciding your legal structure is a decision that becomes increasingly difficult to reverse as a business grows. Pair this with some of the problems we identi-fied in the chapter on advisers, and you realise that entrepreneurs are often not technically equipped to ask the right questions either.

Take a step back and consider how much thought has been put into the structure of your business against the backdrop of where you plan on being five, ten or twenty years from now. Without wanting to dwell on the basics, you will be aware of the available options, ranging from self-employed, limited company (Ltd), limited liability partnership (LLP) and so on.

This is likely to have been decided following a conversation with the company accountant. The deciding factors tend to circle around topics such as: nature of business, growth plans, hiring plans, and taxation. However, businesses evolve, pivot and grow where the rules of engagement are constantly changing. In a lot of cases, the final decision cannot be arrived at after following a simple decision tree to a particular answer.

For example, in certain cases it might make no sense from an income and cost perspective to be a limited company, but the nature of the business alone warrants adequate legal protection. For example, in a food business you probably wouldn't want to be personally accountable (as a self-employed person) in case someone were to have a nasty reaction to your food.

On the other end of the spectrum, it may make sense for a certain venture to operate via a limited company but as there are multiple partners an LLP would ultimately provide better governance, eg a consultancy or professional services firm – you want the flexibility to be able to add and remove partners with ease, while each partner is legally protected from the actions of the others.

As a result, it is truly in the entrepreneur's interest to be educated in business structures so that proactive decisions can be taken if the legacy structure has or will become outdated. Here are some examples of matters that should trigger a company review. If the company is:

- Initiating a revenue stream that carries a different VAT rate to regular revenue

- Experiencing changes to its risk profile

- Purchasing a business property

- Now selling overseas

- Establishing multiple sub-brands / product lines

- Seeking to sell equity to outside investors

- Considering taking on debt finance

Naturally, no adviser is close enough to the business to be able to foresee some of these events unless you develop a culture of including them in every decision. Often, entrepreneurs may proceed on any one of the above without realising the structure of the business may benefit from being evolved to accommodate such decisions. Whether this means migrating from self-employed to Ltd or Ltd to LLP or LLP back to Ltd is a level of technical knowledge that you should defer to your advisers but a conversation that should be initiated internally. The chief of a high-growth start-up is only going to be wise to these requirements if they have spent the time studying the nuances. In the absence of this education, you rely heavily on an open channel of communication with your accountant.

To summarise the considerations that should be taken into account when deciding, we have provided a summary of thoughts at www.thefinancedepartment.co.

Documentation

Throughout the life of any company, there will be important documents that will remain relevant at every stage. Typically, these are a combination of registrations and confirmatory notices issued by HMRC and/or Companies House. You are likely to need any or all of these documents for the following purposes:

- Opening a bank account

- Opening a credit account with a supplier

- Passing anti-money laundering requirements for counterparties

- Legal due diligence undertaken by a potential investor or acquirer

- Registering for HMRC online services

These documents may include:

- Company incorporation documents (incorporation certificate, memorandum of understanding, article of association, register of directors, register of members/shareholders)

- Company corporation tax certificate (CT41G)

- Company VAT certification

- Company PAYE/accounts reference number

- Directors' identification documents – typically a passport

Create a dedicated folder both physically and on the company server where this can be accessed at all times. This will form an integral part of what we will later refer to as the Finance Bible.

You will find that members of the marketing department require these documents as often as the finance and management team. Some of the documents will date back to when the company was first set up and it's not fun for anybody to have to ask the CEO to trawl through an old Hotmail inbox to find the original documents. Putting together a structured system of all of the above documents is a hallmark of a company that is preparing to 'grow up' and mature into a resilient business. It may seem like an hour's work to put this together but the circumstances under which these documents are requested often lead to delays if the company is unable to produce them instantly. It also provides an immediate insight into the credibility of a company's processes, discipline and maturity.

Team

For any high-growth start-up, hiring will be one of your earliest and most consistent challenges. Every hire must be a good fit personally, financially and culturally. As part of the growing up process, one of the fundamental requirements of a successful implementation is having team members in key positions who have charted this course before and are therefore more experienced than you.

Growing up here means letting go. Accepting that once you have made a decision to hire senior specialists in their field, you (as CEO/founder) will no longer have day-to-day management of that particular function. If you are not 100% comfortable with this, you have not found the right candidate. Alternatively, if you find yourself incapable of evolving your hierarchy this way, maybe you are not inclined to be the CEO of a 'grown up' business.

A key hire at this stage is someone to lead the finance team. The head of finance, CFO or finance director will be tasked with oversight of anything involving numbers. They are likely to be a superhero and scapegoat in equal measure, depending on the day. Critically, the individual hired in this role should have exponentially more knowledge about finance and accounting than the CEO. This means that the more finance orientated the CEO is, the deeper the CFO's technical and commercial ability should be.

Note that your dream management team is a set of complimentary skillsets, not sub-divisions of tasks the CEO doesn't have time to do. This is a key distinction often lost on many management teams.

In a fast-growing company, the CFO should be equipped to take responsibility for the journey ahead. While the rest of the company will be focused on growth at all costs, the finance team's primary role is to keep up and support while ensuring the business is compliant, organised and efficient. This unique vantage point means the right character will need to continuously balance the needs of the company commercially while sufficiently satisfying the needs of all the key stakeholders. This is a difficult role and can often cause a divide between the CFO and their colleagues.

This friction is necessary. Embrace it.

Look at the following table showing a thorough list of required attributes when hiring a finance lead.

Finance lead – job responsibilities and attributes	
Responsibilities	Implement and own the processes around internal controls, KPIs and forecasting
	Be lead author of internal Finance Bible
	Design roles and responsibilities to be retained in-house versus outsourced
	Design and recruit finance team
	Liaise with key stakeholders – HMRC, investors and the board
	Recruit team of advisers and liaise with them to ensure regulatory compliance including all statutory and tax filings
	Lead the business through forthcoming fundraising processes
	Work alongside the tech team to assist with designing possible finance back office modules
	Design training and development for the whole firm on finance processes

Continued

Finance lead – job responsibilities and attributes	
Required skills and experience	Qualified accountant
	Experience of having worked in a company that has scaled rapidly, preferably a start-up
	Experience of having led more than £1 million in fundraising
	Keen eye for detail
	Strong IT skills, particularly Excel; experience with data analytics tools is a bonus
	Ability to challenge assumptions and working processes
	Passion for developing people through work
	Existing relationships with advisers and specialists would be beneficial

Finding one stellar CFO is better than hiring multiple inexperienced juniors in their place. A quality leader will be familiar with quick-win efficiencies, systems and short cuts that no amount of extra hands could replicate.

The following figure shows a structure that many high-growth companies have implemented with long-term success. Naturally, with the number of individuals required, this structure is likely to only be afforded by those who have secured adequate funding to do so.

The finance department is centrally structured in the company with direct input and influence on every other department.

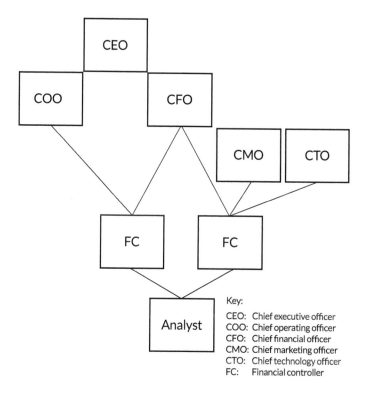

Key:

CEO: Chief executive officer
COO: Chief operating officer
CFO: Chief financial officer
CMO: Chief marketing officer
CTO: Chief technology officer
FC: Financial controller

In the diagram, members of the finance function are positioned to regularly interact with leaders of other departments and translate that learning into strategic actions for the leadership team. While it might be great that the fortress has many 'decision rooms', there should only be one central 'war room' against which all decisions are aligned. This instils a culture of accountability and ensures that first principles such as profitability, cashflow management and governance resound across the organisation. This simple change will instantly improve a company's efficiency, and performance reports will naturally begin to reflect structural benefits where they may have ordinarily highlighted a list of problems in need of fixing.

At a board meeting, it is far more powerful to say: 'Rachel, our financial controller, assisted our CTO with the roll out of the tech plan, so you can see we have aligned the last three months' spend with our cashflow KPIs,' than to say: 'Unfortunately, we have overspent on tech over the course of the last three months, but we are actively working to ensure this does not happen moving forwards.'

Growing up is rooted in effective capital and human resource allocation. This is also one of the primary reasons why the CFO should be tasked with designing training and development for fellow executive management members. It is important that each department is driven and reported against a stakeholder within the finance team. Not only does this promote a culture of data-driven strategy, it also ensures there is a unified approach to growth within the company.

In-house vs outsourcing

One of the first projects a newly hired finance lead should take on is a review of all the tasks that are performed internally against what has been delegated to external advisers. Now that a growth plan has been established, it may be an appropriate time to assess whether it is more productive/cost effective to bring more 'in-house' or even the opposite, to outsource more. This decision inevitably needs to be based on the resources available within the finance team against the required time and competence to complete those tasks effectively.

The split is usually as follows:

In-house	Outsourced
Customer invoicing	Book-keeping
Receipt management	Submit VAT returns
Payments	Process payroll liabilities
a) Suppliers	a) Submit RTI (Real Time Information) to HMRC
b) Salaries	
Debtor chasing	b) Submit pension details
	c) Issue payslips to staff
	Annual statutory accounts
	Annual corporation tax return
	Company secretarial work
	P11d submissions
	EMI (Enterprise Management Incentives) submissions
	R&D (Research and Development) tax credits

It stands to reason that the finance leads' own bandwidth should be consumed with as little 'labour' as possible. Their focus is to help drive the business forwards using their expertise in ways the wider management team cannot. The above tasks should therefore be categorised and managed in accordance with the cost benefit analysis of each option – eg even if it is cost effective to outsource our payroll, is it more meaningful for us to be close to the detail of our staff members' monthly remuneration?

For high-performing companies, I have seen the split of activities as follows:

Finance lead	Advisers	Finance team
KPI reporting	Prepare and file accounts	Daily book-keeping
Financial modelling	Prepare and submit corporation tax	Preparation of VAT return
Board reporting	Prepare and submit EMI submissions	Preparation of monthly payroll
Architect of processes	Prepare and submit R&D tax credits	Preparation of management accounts
	Review and submit VAT	Prepare annual P11d filings
	Review and submit payroll	

Training

In an ever-evolving global landscape, small businesses run the risk of becoming insular and cut off from channels of knowledge. It is therefore incumbent upon the management team to ensure there is a mechanism by which staff, particularly in finance, are continuously training. For many qualified professionals, this will be a prerequisite of their institutes but for the wider company there is no such obligation, and an initiative must be designed.

There will be industry-specific training that certain regulated companies will need to prioritise but as a rule all finance departments as well as other key management personnel should be continuously updated on the following matters:

- Anti-money laundering laws
- Health and safety
- General Data Protection Regulation (GDPR)
- Ethics for business
- Unconscious bias, racism, diversity and inclusion

The above topics are relevant to all business leaders and a truly progressive company will ensure all staff members are collectively benefitting from and assessed against these standards.

Culture

A fundamental shift that founders often struggle with is recognising that the company they started through their own hard work and determination is now no longer their proprietary 'plaything'. When a company decides to take on staff and investors who are invested in the long-term success of the business, it evolves into a shared narrative that everybody is contributing towards. Along the way, further stakeholders join the journey but you, as the primary player in setting it up, can now no longer leverage that influence on how the company governs itself financially. This lesson is ignored at your peril and carries deep-rooted consequences.

The idea that the company must function and abide by a homogenous set of rules is good governance 101. However, you (as the founder) and the CFO (as the designer) are the orchestrators and chief example setters of this behaviour. This means that simple processes such as claiming expenses are in place as much for the CEO as they are for the intern. Founders who ignore this part of the growing up process short-change the chances of the entire organisation evolving into an efficient engine. As a consequence, there is almost always a resentment that permeates throughout the workforce, undermining the processes as well as the legitimacy of the founder as a steward of a business that aspires to be well run.

Other than the process of claiming expenses, below are some other common examples of how founders can undermine the organisation's governance:

- Claiming certain personal expenses should be borne by the company, eg meals

- Ensuring all authorisations pass through them, eg all bank payments

- Not seeking input from the finance team or advisers when entering into new business relationships

Any founder not committed to eradicating such behaviour is fundamentally not fit to lead a well-structured organisation. It is the equivalent of asking your team to tirelessly build a fortress while you yourself regularly forget to lock the doors, turn the lights off and turn the alarm on. It is dangerous, frustrating and immature. Growing up is an inflection point at which you dispense with many of the habits that got you to that point in exchange for a new blueprint that the entire organisation operates from. This makes it hard for founders to concede to this discipline in the first place; they believe it will blunt the 'secret sauce' that makes them who they are. As well as this, scarring caused by paying for disparate and disjointed advice over the years from ill-suited advisers and other entrepreneurs leads to an innate sense of scepticism and reluctance to blindly concede.

With all of these factors at play, the need of the hour does not change and must be embraced with urgency.

Summary

- Becoming a mature, grown up company is not an entitlement, nor does it automatically happen through the passage of time - you must earn it.

- The success of this evolutionary process must be embraced by the entire organisation but particularly the most senior officials.

- Commit to the same vision but recognise this comes from everyone doing their own job well. The finance leadership should regularly be at odds with colleagues from around the business if they are doing their job properly.

- Ensure the finance leadership plays a central role within and around the business for better outcomes.

- Design a training programme for the wider organisation to understand the things that matter to the finance function.

- Recognise you might not be the right person to lead the company through every stage of its growth.

5

The Finance Bible – The Heart Of Your Finance Function

At the heart of your finance function should be a living, breathing document that outlines all the company's financial details. From basic administrative information such as the Companies House registration number and VAT number to specific monthly and quarterly accounting entries that need to be added into the book-keeping software.

Other than efficient governance, the document is designed to survive any number of staff members who may join and leave the organisation. True resilience is to be unaffected by these changes and treat them as expected and predictable. Documentation of how the business operates allows for incoming personnel to simply carry on from where predecessors will have left off. A lot of inefficiency in early-stage businesses stems from a dependence on intellectual capital that is carried within key individuals. The quicker this knowledge can be immortalised into policy, the quicker the company can be deemed to have 'grown up'.

A full template of the Finance Bible can be found at www.thefinancedepartment.co.

Who is it for?

Everyone. From a new joiner all the way to the chief executive, this document will serve as a source of truth and testament to effective governance. It is vital to constantly update it as matters change and new information and processes are adopted. To ensure that the company is always moving in the same direction, it is also prudent to ensure that the CFO is the 'owner' of the document – its accuracy and relevance should form part of their appraisal and ongoing performance criteria.

Every new joiner should be encouraged to read this document upon joining the company. It may seem a little obscure to have the new marketing graduate be forced to read a document that highlights mundane facts like when the company's VAT quarters end but we are trying to achieve an appreciation for these concepts across the company. It is a net benefit to the organisation as a whole if even one small detail of the document can lead to a cashflow benefit, eg a marketing invoice is paid before the end of the month as the head of marketing knew that the VAT quarter end was looming and thus the outlay could be reclaimed.

The evolving nature of the document requires members of the finance team to continuously articulate these concepts in coherent language, which reinforces their own understanding of how well concepts and processes are being internally understood. Promoting this model of thinking helps a growing business in immeasurable ways.

What is it for?

On a basic level, the Finance Bible serves as a quick reference guide for someone who might need the company VAT number, as well as a step-by-step manual on how to claim expenses within the business, without having to ask for assistance.

More substantially, the document serves as a statement of intent from the management that there is a framework designed for the wellbeing of the company and everyone associated with it. In the fortress, this would be equivalent to a document charting the rules of engagement, the code to which the structure adheres, eradicating the need for micromanagement and enabling individuals to be self-sufficient. This level of organisation in early-stage businesses provides staff and potential investors with confidence when it is needed most. It alleviates any ambiguity within the organisation and ensures that there are coherent, repeatable processes that can at any time be checked and reconciled.

Having seen multiple businesses scale from operating in the spare bedroom to being acquired for large sums of money, I can attest to some of the following benefits to this approach that might not be obvious in the early stages:

- Helps provide an audit trail for transactions that are queried in the future

- Sets a positive tone for any due diligence process undertaken by a potential investor or acquirer

- Provides a good impression at the start of any tax investigation

- Enforces a level of discipline throughout the organisation that has knock-on benefits into other departments and processes

- Provides a measurable framework against which to appraise staff members

- Minimises human error

- Lowers statutory audit fees when it becomes mandatory for the company to undertake one

- Allows non-technical staff to operate finance function in an emergency

The document

The document should aim to do three things:

1. **Teach:** Ensure the Finance Bible is written in universally understandable language. Not only is this a good method to ensure it is understood by the finance staff themselves, it also ensures there is no confusion on the part of non-technical teammates. A by-product of this document should be a collective improvement in understanding of why these processes are important, rather than just rote learning of two-dimensional rules. The CFO should take responsibility for the language to achieve this.

2. **Remind:** The utilisation of and adherence to the Finance Bible and its processes will be a direct function of the example set by senior management. A mature business can no longer be operated at the whim of the founders, with one rule for them and another for everybody else. This behaviour becomes toxic and a source of resentment, which ultimately undermines the company. The Finance Bible should therefore also serve as a reference book to senior staff on what processes must be followed in every circumstance, even if they have the ability or discretion to undertake the same task quicker through non-compliance.

3. **Protect:** The Finance Bible becomes a constitutional document within an organisation and serves to protect the interests of its stakeholders. The cost of human error or cavalier financial governance within small businesses is immeasurable. These errors are largely seemingly harmless, eg charging an expense claim to 'travel' rather than 'entertainment', but the systematic documentation of processes limits these as well as more deliberate errors. The Finance Bible serves to minimise the number of seemingly harmless errors that quietly compound to hamper the potential of any organisation. You only need to go through the process of financial due diligence once to realise how silly these errors end up looking when you're trying to get acquired.

Below are some of the chapters your Finance Bible should cover:

1. Company profile

2. Advisers and contact details

3. Software map

4. Roles and responsibilities

5. Company-specific adjustments

6. Dates and deadlines

7. Policies

8. Other notes

Company profile

This is a top sheet, outlining every small detail of the company, eg unique tax references and VAT number so that they can be used internally as well as provided to anyone who might need them such as lawyers/accountancy firms. To help fresh recruits, this section highlights exactly what the business does and how that links into the governance structure that has been designed, eg 'We are a regulated business – we must be able to account for every penny'.

Advisers and contact details

A company will employ a number of advisers at any one time. This will typically include accountants and lawyers. It is vital that all their details such as partner name, telephone number, email address, services provided to your company and so on are itemised. It is also handy to map out the advisers so that a new employee can easily see where each firm fits into the company's day-to-day operations. A short explanation of the scope of each engagement will ensure that any new reader will not struggle to understand what role each adviser plays.

Software map

An impactful adviser will always recommend a suite of software and technology that you should be using.

To easily capture how all of these operate, it is worth drawing a software map that visualises where each system fits into the company's operations. The aim of this illustration is to ensure any new joiner can instantly understand the flow of processes across software.

With a wide variety of applications available, it is possible that some are able to connect to each other, whereas others may not. This type of information is critical to document so that the whole company is aware of where physical intervention is required in the process.

In an ideal world, the usernames and passwords for all of these would also be included here but, for security reasons, a companywide password manager should be utilised.

Roles and responsibilities

The finance department is unique in having to balance specific statutory deadlines as well as ensure future planning and forecasting is undertaken to assist with decision making.

It is vital that every individual in the finance department is aware of their responsibilities within an organisation. However, for this to be a worthwhile exercise it is just as relevant for them to know what their team members are responsible for. This should not be a replication of the job description but rather a mutually agreed scope that precisely itemises the company-specific tasks. After agreeing this scope, there should be no margin for ambiguity about where responsibilities lie. It is just as useful for members of other departments to know this as those within finance; for example, it is inefficient for the head of marketing to be requesting a performance report from a team member who is not involved in that process.

In some instances, a company may not have the luxury of multiple individuals within finance. Here, it is even more important to ensure that the document is kept up to date and the divide between work carried out internally and outsourced is outlined. Accountancy firms will often refer to this document as a 'statement of work' or a 'document of understanding', though where this is not available an internal version should be created. As advisers we often find ourselves meeting replacement heads of finance in early-stage businesses who walk into their roles with no guidance or legacy processes left behind by their predecessors.

Company-specific adjustments

This will be unique to every company, but it is critical that the finance team are aware of exactly what they are. For example, in a software as a service business, what percentage of funds held at the bank represent a liability for services not yet provided? Similarly, what is the company depreciation policy for fixed assets?

All of these combined are known as the 'period-end journals' and are vital for transforming a set of numbers into a meaningful document for analysis. Some examples include:

- Depreciation

- Deferred income

- Deferred tax

- Contingent liabilities

- Accruals

- Pre-payments

- Bad debts

- Revaluations and impairments

Dates and deadlines

There will be a number of deadlines, both internal and external. A comprehensive calendar of deliverables and reporting dates should be available for everyone to refer to. Everything from when filings are due to when tax payments must be made should be hard coded for referencing at any point.

Policies

Some of the first administrative problems a new joiner will often face are how to claim for expenses and how to book annual leave. The newer the business, the more acute this problem is and there is plenty of excellent software available to tackle these issues. This section of the Finance Bible should ensure there is no ambiguity with regards to what the company policy and process is. Below are some examples of such policies that a company should consider having documented:

- Expense claiming

- Holiday requesting

- Time off in lieu and/or overtime

- Working from home

- Travel expenses – what is claimable and at what rate

Statutory file

This is a legal register of the Directors and Shareholders of the business as well as a summary of all of the updates made to the company since its inception.

See 'Effective Fundraising – The Minimal Viable Processes' (Chapter 11).

Other

This document needs to serve the purposes of your organisation, so the 'other' section could serve as a place to add additional notes or it could be renamed eg 'Bank Accounts', listing all company accounts, their details, branch details and specific uses. A lot will depend on how many people within the organisation have access to each section and how much detail you wish to include.

Keep it up to date

It is recommended that the head of finance 'owns' this document for obvious reasons. However, it is the responsibility of the entire organisation to ensure the finance department is informed of any changes that need to be made. For this reason, the naming convention of the document should always include the date at which it was last updated by the responsible person.

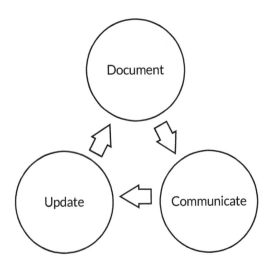

Unless the organisation can rely on this document blindly, it will not fulfil its purposes. The goal is to limit the need for unnecessary questions, searching through email inboxes and confirming basic details. Over time, your company will notice this translates into operational efficiency. These are the real wins that a good CFO will prioritise.

Summary

- Commit to producing and maintaining a Finance Bible that documents the most pertinent information about the company and its processes. It will serve to teach, remind and protect the entire organisation.

- Documentation as a practice encourages consistency and compliance without the need for micromanagement. It is the only way a high-growth company can scale with confidence.

- The Financial Bible should be kept up to date with a nominated person responsible for its maintenance. Either do it properly, or not at all. Bad documentation can sometimes do more damage than none at all.

6
Stakeholders – Who Is Watching You?

M any entrepreneurs cannot concisely articulate who their stakeholders are.

The dictionary definition of stakeholder is 'a person or company that is involved in a particular organization, project, system, etc., especially because they have invested money in it'.[3]

Traditionally, society has ascribed the term stakeholder primarily to those with a financial commitment to an organisation. Over time and through the advent of globalisation and technology, this definition has evolved to capture, more holistically, the impact an organisation has beyond those who use it as a mechanism of generating

---

3   Oxford Learner's Dictionaries, www.oxfordlearnersdictionaries. com/definition/english/stakeholder, accessed 25 June 2021

returns. As a minimum, stakeholders are considered to include: customers, employees, investors, suppliers, communities and government, for example.

It is important for management, particularly the finance department, to be deeply aware of any additional groups that specifically apply to their organisation. An additional list compiled from a cohort of early-stage start-ups could be:

- Regulatory bodies, eg FCA, Air Travel Organiser's Licence (ATOL)

- Natural environment surrounding any physical locations such as parks, lakes, natural habitats, eg the emissions from the factory of a start-up alcohol brand

- Construction Industry Training Board (CITB)

Understanding the environment a company operates in allows the finance department to fine-tune processes, metrics and operations. This is particularly important as each stakeholder group has different rights and expectations from the business but ultimately, the relationship will always be two-way. It is incumbent upon the company to know what duty of care the organisation has to each group and ensure that every member of the finance team understands this explicitly.

This is an interesting exercise to undertake as many of the demands placed upon businesses are usually considered by-products of having robust systems and processes. The finance function is the engine room from which all efficiencies across the organisation start. If finance is world-class, there's a good chance the other departments will be too. If finance is mediocre, all other departments will at best be mediocre.

It is telling when any of the items listed below are met with negative attitudes as to what that might say about the internal dynamics of a company.

The two-way relationship of each stakeholder

	Company to stakeholder	Stakeholder to customer
Customers	A desired product or service	Source of revenue
	Customer service and feeling of importance	Strongest source of advocacy to other potential customers
Employees	Salary/livelihood	The collective benefit of years of education and experiences
	Equity	
	Source of pride purpose and impact	Physical assistance with performing a role that contributes to the company achieving its larger objectives
	Platform for future prosperity	
		Commitment of time at the expense of alternative career options available to them

Continued

The two-way relationship of each stakeholder (cont.)

	Company to stakeholder	Stakeholder to customer
Investors	Opportunity to partake in the ownership and therefore future economic upside of the business or project	Investment funds. Collective benefit of experience and stewardship, assisting the company in areas where they may not have experience Strongest advocate for the company in the eyes of future investors and customers
Suppliers	Source of revenue for the supplier Advocate of supplier's products or services to other customers (provided there are no trade secrets preventing this)	Source of key components that allow the business to generate economic value Critical partner in the supply chain to ensure the company is able to meet customer demands
Communities	Providing jobs and prosperity to the local area – in some cases Providing obstruction to the local community – in other cases	Providing a home for the company to operate in A source of local talent from which to employ people Strong advocacy as community takes pride in local company

Continued

The two-way relationship of each stakeholder (cont.)

	Company to stakeholder	Stakeholder to customer
Government	Timely and accurate reporting to various departments eg HMRC, Companies House, Innovate UK/Scotland, local council, Department of Trade and industry	Providing the conditions and framework within which a business can safely and securely operate Assistance via grants, favourable loans and subsidies

The two-way relationship of each stakeholder

We will focus on the main six categories of stakeholder and the role your finance department plays:

1. Customers

2. Employees

3. Investors

4. Suppliers

5. Communities

6. Government

Customers

Customers are the stakeholders who form the bottom row on the house of cards. Keeping them satisfied as a business is fundamentally driven by the quality of the core product or service being provided. However, you will often see businesses win or lose customers on the strength of their customer service and/or administrative processes. Amazon is a good example of this – their keen focus on the customer experience has created a deep sense of loyalty and trust in the eyes of their most important stakeholder. Designing, implementing, and championing this culture starts with the finance team. The rigidity with which processes and guidelines are adhered to makes customer-centricity a by-product. Some examples of instances where a sharp finance team can impress a potential customer:

- Ability to instantly provide an up-to-date customer balance/statement for businesses where credit is extended

- A thorough understanding of the different VAT rates that apply to different scenarios ie business to business, UK to Europe, UK to USA, as they are often different

- Instantly being able to relay stock levels of individual products when customers request them via an accurate dashboard of inventory

Employees

In my house of cards example, if anyone could share the bottom row with customers it would be this stakeholder group. For employees, having a robust finance team is as much an occupational perk as it is a necessity. Early-stage businesses are plagued with uncertainty, through a variety of entirely uncontrollable reasons. It is therefore the job of the management team to ensure that the working environment is one where simple things are executed impressively well, so that it becomes part of the attraction of working there. The average employee is likely to swing between needing the finance function for personal reasons (salary, holiday, benefits) and needing it to deliver on their job role. Many administrative processes are highlighted in the Finance Bible but the department's ability to assist employees in their jobs is a competitive advantage that only the best early-stage businesses grasp. We will discuss this in more detail later.

Investors

Psychologically, it is important to understand that investors should never and will never want anything from your business that you shouldn't want or need for yourself.

Over the life of a business, a company may encounter different types of investor. Initially, they may be non-interfering friends and family; this may progress to institutional/professional investors as the company's needs grow. One thing that will not change is the role of the finance function in being the part of the business that is responsible for their wellbeing and requests. Like all other stakeholders, investors will want the finance function to be well organised, efficient and productive, although professional investors may place specific demands upon the company.

To better understand this dynamic, it is important to delve into the factors at play. Professional investors are usually deemed 'professional' by virtue of the fact they are investing other people's money. They will often contractually have committed themselves to obtaining regular financial updates from their portfolio companies so they can report back to their ultimate investor. The recipients of professional investment (ie you) should ensure that the reporting processes, Finance Bible, frameworks and outputs are optimised to deliver to these needs. While the company will be satisfying a contractual requirement in providing this reporting, reports and data of this nature should be by-products of how your finance function has been set up, regardless of who is asking for them.

As well as reporting on performance, a positive attitude towards processes and financial competitive advantage is an alluring credential to not only attract investors but also help in making those investors ambassadors for the company to future investors.

This is critical to successful fundraising dynamics as well as ensuring that the capital ecosystem in which your business operates has a positive representation of the inner workings of your company.

Suppliers

Arguably all that matters is that they are paid on time and deliver the product or service that you have engaged them for. Peel away from this objective and dismissive headline and it doesn't take long to realise that supplier efficiency is vital to you being able to deliver to your customers. Whether that is the raw material that is used in making your product or the hosting service upon which your website is built, your business expects flawless service to the point of taking it for granted.

At a base level, this relationship is established through day-to-day interactions, typically on administrative matters such as invoicing, deliveries, refunds and credit statements. Over time the efficiency with which these matters are resolved becomes the bedrock for how you as a customer are perceived. The ability to produce documents, invoices and statements is a function of a well organised book-keeping process, underpinned by the Finance Bible and appropriately set up software. Strict discipline in this regard not only assists with keeping accurate records but also helps with future negotiations with suppliers. The best early-stage businesses recognise this early and use it as leverage to negotiate the best terms with suppliers on the strength of the relationship developed through simple interactions. This is an example where the finance function can visibly contribute towards better profitability for the business.

Communities

In thinking about communities, it is prudent to include any body, institution or group that falls within the company's orbit. While the local convenience store may be in no way impacted by your daily existence, it falls within your community simply by proximity. It is also advisable for a company to be clear about exactly who falls into this category and what responsibilities you have to each other.

It is your responsibility to be considered a worthy member of this community through your actions, governance and contribution. For companies this is sometimes measured through the level of tax they pay or the frequency with which they deliver projects via corporate social responsibility initiatives. A key tenet of this role is that it cannot be faked and there is no right formula to follow. It is the responsibility of key management to implement how the company will behave to ensure its role in the wider community is regarded as a net contributor. As stewards of the company's resources, the finance function should play a pivotal role in defining this strategy as well as ensure that wider stakeholder groups are consciously made aware of these efforts.

Government

At any given time, your company will have multiple personalities in the eyes of the government. As a result, it is likely that the company will have dialogue with at least the following departments:

- HMRC

- Department of Work and Pensions

- Local council

- Valuations Office - Business rates

- Innovate UK and/or Innovate Scotland

It is these relationships that tend to worry management the most, primarily because the fear of error has real and immediate consequences that have haunted businesses through time. While it is critical that the company's scorecard is 'clean' in the eyes of the government, it is unlikely that the tax office or anyone else will demand anything from you that you shouldn't aspire to have anyway.

Given HMRC is likely to be the most prominent institution the company interacts with, it is worth spending some time understanding this dynamic. From the outset the company's relationship with HMRC will evolve from fairly 'light touch' to predictably frequent. Upon incorporation, the company is registered simply with the corporation tax department, who will issue a Unique Tax Reference number via a CT41G form. Every year, upon filing of the accounts, it is expected that a commensurate corporation tax return will be filed, outlining the profit or loss position and the tax payable thereon.

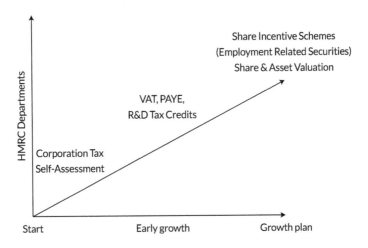

These are the primary stages:

- **Start:** corporation tax, self-assessment

- **Early growth:** VAT, PAYE, R&D tax credits

- **Growth plan:** share and asset valuation, share incentive scheme (employment related securities)

As the company grows and takes on more responsibility, it will take on greater compliance obligations to additional departments within the tax office. Any one of those departments has the liberty to launch an enquiry into the accuracy of reporting for their specific tax as well as across the board, if they so choose. It is this possibility that defines many of the processes we deem to be critical. Ultimately, through strict compliance with the framework we have defined for success, a natural by-product is the ability to satisfy any investigation by the tax authorities.

Another aspect of the finance function's relationship with the government is to ensure it is up to date with the latest legislation, advice, grants and announcements. This information is often disseminated through word of mouth, passed along through a series of conversations ultimately resulting in an email or phone call to the accountants. It is vital that the head of finance or CFO is subscribed to appropriate information sources for the stage and industry that the company operates in (eg signing up to www.thefinancedepartment.co).

The company's access to knowledge is usually directly correlated with their accountants' willingness to keep them informed. This creates a disadvantage for companies that may benefit from certain announcements or could do with warning against any imminent changes in applicable legislation. Obtaining this information in a timely, accurate manner is the responsibility of the finance department. Further still, it is incumbent upon the finance department to digest and implement any changes that may benefit or affect the company without waiting to be informed.

Summary

- Undertake an exercise to map all of your stakeholders to ensure you know exactly who they are.

- Customers and employees are the most fundamental stakeholders to your operation.

- Stakeholders across the board cannot be served if the business is not underpinned by an efficient finance function.

- As the company grows, it will increasingly fall under the radar of additional HMRC offices and external stakeholders such as the public. Ensure that your finance function operates in conjunction with those responsibilities, rather than behaving reactively.

7
Metrics – How Is Your Business Scoring?

A common management adage is, 'What gets measured gets managed.' This is a simple concept that speaks less to mathematics but more to a culture of constant improvement.

To enable a business to do this successfully, the critical drivers of value must be clear to the leadership team and beyond. Many small businesses never get to the point where they can reliably analyse their performance, as their fundamental processes (book-keeping, regularity, reporting) are never optimised to a suitable standard. It's no wonder this chapter is preceded by so many others; without them, there's no point talking about metrics.

Assuming the company financials are being updated regularly, metrics should be reported alongside period management accounts. These are often produced monthly and quarterly for the benefit of management as well as investors. I recommend that businesses begin viewing their financial statements through the lens of these metrics as early as possible. After all, what do statutory financial statements even mean unless they are brought to life with some colour, context, perspective and comparison?

Why is measuring metrics important?

To begin thinking about this, it's worth looking around you and your daily life and how many inherent 'metrics' you rely upon as a given. While it may be hugely exciting to drive your car non-stop across the country, you would be nervous if I asked you to do it without your fuel, oil and radiator gauges – or how about your speedometer? Using this example, you can start to form a picture of what purpose metrics serve in a business setting. They are there to serve, protect and guide you in a way that enables you to make 'good' decisions.

On a more sophisticated level, these insights allow you to seek competitive advantages as well as assist with identifying emerging opportunities and threats. Therefore, no two businesses will be measuring the same criteria. Every industry is unique and within every industry each individual business has nuances that guide priorities and associated metrics.

How to think about metrics in the early days

At the very inception of your business, it will often feel meaningless to 'track' against a series of targets and metrics that look more like fiction than a reality. This could not be further from the truth, if you are willing to be tough on yourself. If nothing else, this exercise, done properly, will tell you whether this business idea is working or not. More importantly, it allows you to harness the ability to iterate plans in the presence of feedback and data. Training your eye to embrace what the numbers are telling you is a discipline that a lot of early-stage founders never develop, often because they didn't start early enough.

On a blank sheet of paper (or a spreadsheet), write down the key components of how your business intends to make money. If you do this in enough detail, using well researched assumptions, you will eventually have put together a financial model for your business. This is the first 'sniff test' for whether your planned journey is realistic or not. In some cases, you won't know until you start trading, but the hard science is to ensure you are adequately tracking your performance against the plans in your forecasts. If all is going seemingly well, great – maybe you need to adjust your assumptions and accelerate faster. If it isn't, consider which elements of your assumptions turned out to be wrong. It is worth reflecting at this point on whether you have misunderstood the importance of this given assumption or if there was something wrong about your execution. Those are really the only two questions you can ask yourself at this point – but will you answer honestly?

CASE STUDY: FINTECH AIN'T CHEAP

A well-known Fintech business had prepared a financial model suggesting that their cost of acquisition (CAC)[4] for any given customer was £94.

On this basis the model suggested that with an average revenue of £350 per customer and negligible direct costs, there would be roughly £256 of gross profit per customer.

However, with a large advertising budget and expensive marketing resources, a CAC of £94 only worked if there were 5,000 customers on the platform – a simple economies-of-scale dilemma.

After year one, with a fully resourced marketing team, the number of customers stood at 1,300, which means the real CAC was £361 or, in other words, loss-making.

Possible ways to interpret this data:

---

4   The cost of acquisition is the full unit expense incurred in converting a member of the public into a customer. This includes advertising costs, salaries and any promotional expenses divided by the total number of customers.

- The company's marketing efforts were ineffective.
- The product is not appealing to as many people as first thought, in which case there are two options:
  - Adapt the product.
  - Continue trying to convince the target audience they are wrong.

The above is a prime example of how relentless processes and tracking of metrics, in this case 'gross margin analysis', can provide insights from the very beginning. It also allows founding teams to ask themselves hard questions as early as possible, before expending too much in time and resources on strategies that clearly aren't working.

Metrics should be calculated to serve you in your decision making. When this practice is ignored or side-lined, it speaks to a worrying character trait within founders. There is a fine line between madness and genius when acting against what the facts might be suggesting but management should be equipped to take that decision fully informed. Some of the largest businesses in the world that we all know and love probably don't have favourable 'metrics' such as 'net profit margin' even to this day. Do they care? That depends on what their goals are but rest assured they are not unaware of the facts, either way.

Do intangible metrics matter to the finance team?

Much success in the technology world is attributed to intangible metrics, ie those performance criteria that the company cannot reliably measure the financial impact of (positive or negative), such as 'followers', 'likes', 'endorsements' and 'page views'. These often fall within the domain of the marketing department, who will try to link the company's cashflows to these results. For some consumer facing social businesses, these may well be the ultimate drivers of value and thus comprise the lion's share of worthwhile metrics.

We are living through an age of commerce where the financial statements can sometimes be the most misleading documents to analyse the health and prospects of a given company. Revenue may be low; profit may be non-existent but monthly engagement could be through the roof – go figure. For a finance department operating in this environment, an understanding of how growth in these areas will eventually drive long-term cashflows and profitability is essential, as stakeholders will need to be convinced and reassured. However, it is also within the domain of the CFO to ensure that the plans and potential remain credible and attainable. After all, user engagement doesn't pay the rent.

The first step in adapting for this is to ensure there is alignment between the marketing and finance departments so that both understand and agree to each other's strategies.

Which metrics apply to your business?

The fundamentals of business do not change, regardless of how 'new age' your idea might be. Founders should re-read the above line until they are blue in the face.

Having said that, the nature of developing cutting-edge technology and business models requires heavy, front-loaded investment in the hope that it is paid back in future. This fact is often misused as a comfort blanket to avoid paying attention to the fundamentals today. Too often, the 'build-phase', 'stealth mode', 'day one' status is another way of saying 'loss-making'. The missing piece in this puzzle is that early-stage businesses are surviving on injected capital, often other peoples. While it is a great privilege to have the trust and support of investors who buy into your vision, as a founder, this should be acknowledged via a ruthless sense of responsibility.

At any given time, the company should be able to produce this basic reporting pack:

1. Current cash position
2. Cashflow forecast

3. Gross margin (revenue minus cost of sales)

4. Contribution margin (gross margin minus marketing costs)

The above metrics are 'table stakes' in poker lingo, regardless of whether you have taken external funding or not. However, most finance professionals will be well versed in the above; it is the interpretation of what picture the figures are painting that separates an effective finance function from a passive one. I recommend that the CFO is forced to write commentary using the following format against every metric:

1. What is the absolute result? What was the same result in the last period? What was your target?

2. What factors influenced this result? What factors caused the change since the last period?

3. What short-term impact does this have on the business? What does this result suggest about the future of the business?

To give an example of the benefits of using this structure, consider the case of an e-commerce health and beauty business that I have the pleasure of working with. Let us focus on their Quarter 2 (2020) management reports during the COVID-19 pandemic, particularly their contribution margin.

METRICS - HOW IS YOUR BUSINESS SCORING?

CASE STUDY: HEALTH AND BEAUTY BUSINESS

Q4 2019: 42%

Q1 2020: 43%

Q2 2020: 21%

- CFO note: contribution margin in Q2 2020 was 21%, down 22% from Q1 and 29% below our target of 50%.
- The COVID-19 pandemic forced us to migrate our online marketing efforts to an agency, given our internal resource was unable to work from home.

A 21% contribution margin left us with £23,665 less cash than our forecasts had allowed for this quarter. At present, this is scheduled to continue into Q3 which will place similar strain on working capital and bring our runway forward by net four months. These results suggest we have a critical weakness in our marketing department with *over-reliance on key individuals* such that the business cannot support itself without them. It is recommended that we focus on *negotiating a pre-agreed retainer with a preferred agency* to use in an emergency. We can then forecast for that cost and ensure the workload is spread evenly between internal and external resource.

What is critical here are the actionable steps that can be taken, having fully absorbed the picture that the figures have painted. Many companies would have stopped at concluding that the pandemic was enough to explain the difference, but the structure of the note forces the CFO to produce insights.

This structure should be used for every point made by the CFO and is easily summarised as:

identify → measure → critically analyse → conclude and recommend

This level of interrogation is important for several reasons but none more important than the fact that every business is unique and requires specific monitoring. For high-growth businesses the 'table stakes' are largely regarded as good housekeeping; the 'real' information and directional indicators lie in the metrics the team have teased out to be meaningful.

A fitting example of this is to put 'cost of acquisition' under the spotlight. As described in my Fintech example, this metric is simply an all-in cost of getting your customer over the line. Dig a little deeper and it quickly becomes evident that, in its simplest form, this calculation is meaningless unless ruthlessly defined and adapted. The absence of this scrutiny is the difference between being on a growth path versus aimlessly walking off a cliff.

At what point in the 'customer funnel' does your company consider an individual to be regarded as a customer? Why at that point? Is it when they're signed up? Or when they start paying? Arguably both are relevant, but which one is more appropriate for what you want that figure to mean? Are the cost inputs tangible to the point where a like-for-like calculation is meaningful? Are you selling your products and services online? Or are you having to make phone calls and arrange meetings to onboard new customers? How do you price the cost of a meeting? Do you include that in the cost of attaining the customer?

Achieving this granularity with all of the KPIs produces a set of 'atomic metrics'. To have broken down each result to its component parts and have a thorough understanding of what they really mean empowers the decision makers within the business to not only confidently discuss reports but also reliably identify areas that require attention. This instils a culture of analysis that ensures management are always asking the right questions in pursuit of effective answers.

While the science of finance is universal, the application to your business must be specific. To tease out the variables that really matter for any given business, management must have a laser focus on the critical success factors for the intended goal. Much of this soul searching should be unearthed in the 'What kind of business are you?' phase, but to translate that into a trackable scorecard one must understand:

- Specific dynamics of the industry, eg average lead times to obtain customers, average cost of acquisition for the industry, how crowded is this market, what is our angle to obtain a competitive advantage, is there a seasonality that impacts cashflow management?

- What figures are vanity metrics that do not serve the mission of the company?

- How much gross profit is required to achieve the funding forecasts outlined to investors? How many customers does that translate to? Are that many customers attainable on the current investment plan?

- What specific metric(s) does the company consider to be unambiguously a gauge of product market fit? Customers? Revenue? Gross profit? Something intangible?

- I have yet not mentioned the more popular parlance of key performance indicators or objectives and key results (OKRs). The confusion and conflation of these two terms is often the root cause of poor metrics management.

Shopify defines KPIs as follows:

> 'A key performance indicator, or KPI for short, is one gauge of how well your business is hitting its performance targets. Profit, sales growth, and employee retention are popular KPIs, but ... your KPIs naturally result from annual business goals you set.'[5]

---

5   'Key performance indicator', Shopify, www.shopify.com/ encyclopedia/key-performance-indicator-kpi

John Doerr defines an OKR as 'a collaborative goal-setting tool used by teams and individuals to set challenging, ambitious goals with measurable results. OKRs are how you track progress, create alignment, and encourage engagement around measurable goals'.[6]

At their essence, OKRs are simply KPIs with context and purpose rather than static uninspiring digits. However, it is important to ensure that the metric being tracked is tagged to an overarching objective the fuels the company mission, otherwise what's the point? To assist with clarity, write it down, so there is no confusion in the reader's mind.

When presented in a thought-provoking report, metrics should instantly provide the reader (be it management, investors or employees) with a directional story of where the company is and where it is headed.

Don't kid yourself

If you get to the point where you can hire the right people and produce a well-oiled reporting framework to monitor your company performance, you are shooting everyone in the foot if you let your own delusion get in the way.

---

6   J Doerr, *Measure What Matters: OKRs: The simple idea that drives 10x growth* (Portfolio, 2018)

Delusion can manifest in many ways but most often it is seen through one of the following:

- Intentionally easy goal setting
- Focusing on vanity metrics that serve no greater purpose
- Believing that growth is good in any form
- Assuming industry standards/averages can be ignored and 'hacked' by your company
- Assuming poor financial results always have a financial solution
- Believing profit is not important for technology companies

By surrounding yourself and the company with intelligent people, investors and advisers, the company can avoid falling into the above trap. However, too often companies will bleed to death because of a CEO or CFO who is simply not willing to accept what the numbers are depicting. If nothing else this chapter should assist with igniting this realisation; as all the numerical work is a simple exercise in basic maths, how the company chooses to react can often end up being the average of the egos in the room.

Summary

- Accounts are just numbers on a page unless they are brought to life against goals, targets, comparatives and variances.

- This should be part of the culture of assessing performance rather than something that is done for reporting purposes only.

- In using these metrics and tools you will seek your competitive advantage as a company.

- The earlier you implement performance tracking, the more powerful your decisions will be.

- Measure what you can purposefully; resist relying on soft data to make hard decisions.

- Remember your business is unique, even in a crowded market, and must have as many company-specific metrics as it does industry-specific.

- Blind belief in the face of hard data is delusion every time, until it isn't.

8
Automation – Let Robots Do It For You

Stewart Butterfield, the CEO and founder of Slack, said, 'There's a lot of automation that can happen that isn't a replacement of humans but of a mind-numbing behavior.'[7]

You don't have to read too deeply into this quote to realise that when the mundane is removed, your mind, colleagues, department and business as a whole are free to think more expansively and creatively about genuine problem solving. Only solving a genuine problem can be classed as 'problem solving', everything else is just work.

---

7   Alex Konrad, 'CEO Stewart Butterfield says Slack is evolving into an "Always-on chief of staff"', *Forbes* (24 April 2017), www.forbes.com/ sites/alexkonrad/2017/04/24/slack-ceo-says-its-becoming-always-on-chief-of-staff, accessed 25 June 2021

Often we are too busy to know whether what we are doing is moving the company forwards, backwards or sideways. In a fast-paced environment, where time and resources are limited, there is little room for 'sideways' or 'backwards'. Talented people shouldn't be spending their time and energy on processes that have a tech-based, lower cost alternative.

The knack is knowing how to use them and what problem you are trying to solve. Some good examples are:

- To save time on repetitive tasks, eg bank reconciliation

- To redirect limited staff members onto tasks that can't be automated, eg replying to customer queries

- To limit errors on repetitive but complex tasks, eg calculating depreciation

- To ensure a specific protocol is followed for each instance of a given process, eg expense claiming

Many companies conflate automation with outsourcing. They are not the same thing. While they both seemingly achieve the saving of time, automation is a culture and ethos, whereas outsourcing is a simple deflection. This is easy to see when analysed through the prism of a high-growth enterprise that plans to exponentially increase volume through either customers or traffic. The workload involved in a simple process without automation is directly multiplied by the increased growth, whereas the inverse is true at a firm that tackles the same task through systems. The cost or 'load' borne by an outsourced solution falls victim to the same inefficient correlation; there are no simple economies at scale and, more worryingly, the risk of error at scale becomes amplified.

These tasks can be significantly or completely replaced with an automated solution:

- Bank reconciliations

- Accounting journal entries

- Invoicing
    - Sales invoices processing
    - Chasing debts
    - Purchase invoices processing

- Staff onboarding

- Expense claiming

- Time recording

- Payroll

- Holiday requesting

- Stock management

When thinking about systems, companies are usually inundated with options. There are platforms and then there are add-on tools. One of the most important decisions the finance department can make is choosing a platform software that will serve as the main engine for the bulk of transaction recording. This decision is also too often made by the same broken logic that founders use when choosing an accountant – it is normally by referral, a recommendation from a family member or friend, with no thought on the suitability for the company.

Platform vs add-on software

To become a standout player in the market, every platform software has tried to bundle the most effective combination of features by their own logic and built their product accordingly. Your platform software should be the 'best-in-class' option for your needs in the following ways:

- Seamless connectivity with your bank (make sure your specific bank has a live feed)

- Seamless connectivity with your payment processing and/or e-commerce platform (eg Stripe, Shopify, Squarespace, etc)

- Payroll

- Multi-currency capability

- Live support

- A wide-reaching add-on integration capability (eg stock management, financial reporting)

The above list of features is not replicable through a tapestry of other software trying to work in parallel with each other. Whatever you choose, make sure the six features above are non-negotiables.

The decision about which platform software you are going to use should be a collaborative effort by the managing team. During this conversation, it should be established what the current requirements of the company are, coupled with what they are likely to be in a few years' time.

A good starting point to understanding the most scalable solution can normally be found by opting for the software that has the largest 'add-on tools' marketplace. While the top six features as discussed above are arguably best performed by platforms, many smaller functions and processes are better executed via add-ons.

Xero Marketplace has 700 add-on tools (ranging from stock management, payroll, CRM, time reporting), while Quickbooks Marketplace has 600 add-on tools.[8]

Nowadays, most add-on providers try their best to integrate with all of the major platforms. Once they reach a certain size, they tend to get acquired by one

---

8   The Xero App Marketplace - www.apps.xero.com

of the major platforms anyway, eg Xero's acquisition of Hubdoc[9] or Quickbooks' acquisition of TSheets.[10] Once you start using them, it becomes evident that most apps are built with one of the major platforms in mind, while remaining connectable to the others.

Once a company reaches a certain size, the cloud-based solutions outlined above become wholly unfit for purpose. While your business does have to reach a substantial scale, there is a case for bespoke enterprise resource planning software such as Sage, Oracle and NetSuite.

CASE STUDY: THE HEAVY INDUSTRY BUSINESS

After seeing adverts for some of the new cloud accounting packages, our client in the manufacturing industry, 'SD', gave me a call to see whether it was finally time to move away from their bespoke but rather old desktop package. SD are a heavy industry business: a lot of machines, a lot of stock, goods coming in and out all day, every day. While the five-year-old software was slow, it was the sole system used for everything from purchase orders to credit notes, for millions of transactions a year, and it worked.

---

9   Asha Barbaschow, 'Xero scoops up Hubdoc in $70 million acquisition', ZDNet (31 July 2018), www.zdnet.com/article/xero-scoops-up-hubdoc-in-70-million-acquisition/, https://techcrunch.com/2017/12/05/intuit-acquires-time-tracking-service-tsheets-for-340m, accessed 25 June 2021
10 F Lardinois, 'Intuit acquires time-tracking service TSheets for $340m', techcrunch (5 December 2017), https://tinyurl.com/6xjcp78t

We undertook a like-for-like analysis of newer, cheaper software that could be 'accessed from anywhere' and was 'not contractually binding' as well as all the other buzz words that are associated with SaaS (software as a service) products. From our research, we found systems that connected to the banks but wouldn't connect to a stock management platform, and where they might connect to that, they weren't capable of linking to the electronic point-of-sale machine.

We concluded that there was no solution that would replicate the ease and output of their 'old and slow' software and fundamentally the client was confusing a technology/hardware problem with a software one.

Four years later and following an overhaul of their servers and internet provider, SD are still using the same desktop software solution with no interest in moving away.

Cloud isn't always the answer – don't feel compelled to think it is.

To decide on the best option for the company, it is best to include members from across the management team of the business as well as the company's advisers and software provider representative. They will be able to give frontline experience of other companies in the same situation as you and the best use cases for implementation. Once a decision has been taken, a software map resembling something like this should be drawn out.

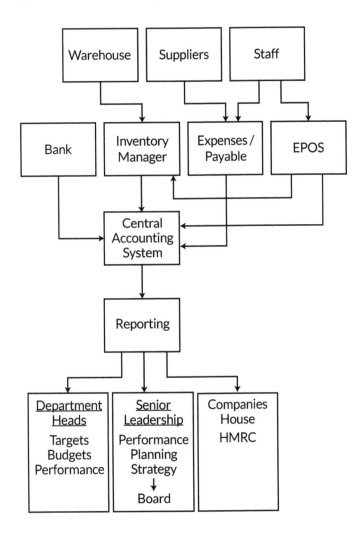

How to get the software working for you

There are many simple automation rules that can be applied to your standard book-keeping software to vastly reduce time and potential for errors (for a list of examples, visit www.thefinancedepartment.co). These pieces of kit were designed to be adapted and customised for your needs so it is well worth spending the time at the front end understanding exactly how much 'work' needs to be physically performed by staff members vs automatically by the software. For example:

- **Auto-coding repetitive expenses** (Amazon, Uber, GSuite): Much like an 'if' function in Excel, all modern accounting software can be adapted to use the same syntax, accounting code and VAT rates for a given supplier, so that in the future it never has to ask you about that again. This can save a lot of time but is often not used by companies due to lack of awareness.

- **Auto-chase unpaid sales invoices after seven days:** In the past, it would have been the responsibility of someone in the accounts department to call or send an email to customers. Most accounting software will now allow you to set up an auto-reminder so this is handled automatically. Nothing revolutionary but all time that can be saved, costs that can be cut and efficiencies that can be capitalised upon.

- **Auto-generation of VAT reports:** A by-product of accurate daily reconciliations should be VAT returns being available at the click of a button. While they won't necessarily be ready to submit (due to adjustments), a good estimate of the company's refund or liability can always be obtained. This ultimately helps with better cashflow forecasting and therefore decision making.

Always automate

Automation is a mindset that senior leadership should always be looking to leverage. It is more than just a weapon by which to achieve cost savings; done properly, it becomes the sole contributor to curbing employee boredom as well as a catalyst to focus on more 'fun' things. Apart from the motivational benefits, this is exactly the headspace you want talented staff members to be channelling their energies towards. Only through systematising the seemingly mundane can a finance team realistically attempt to focus on the useful and productive elements of the business.

Dashboards

The purpose of affording yourself the luxury of time and freeing yourself of the monotonous is to allow the team to double down on what matters. Defining the seemingly useful and productive is discussed in the metrics chapter of this book but let's say for the sake of argument that the real critical success factors for your business have been decided as: maintaining a gross profit margin of 47% and ensuring cost of acquisition does not exceed £130. The whole mantra of automation is only worth it if these numbers are set up to be calculated automatically via a dashboard.

As a company, it is likely that over time, some form of management reporting pack will need to be designed, whether that is for the benefit of the senior leadership or to present to the board of directors on a frequent basis. There is no right answer to what level of information should be provided in these packs as the best ones are designed to be tailored to what matters to that specific company. Taking an automated dashboard approach to conveying the metrics that matter helps with focusing the minds and efforts of the entire team.

Some of the most efficient companies we have worked with cultivate this habit by circulating these numbers via an email summary to the senior leadership at the end of the day. If you are responsible for marketing and the numbers around cost of acquisition are beginning to creep outside the required range, the rest of the company will expect you to have some answers. There are tools available that will display this information in a meaningful yet light touch way, some of which you can see at www.thefinancedepartment.co, although instilling these habits via a spreadsheet is always a good place to start.

The case for outsourcing

Outsourcing is a misdirected automation opportunity. At its core, automation strives to guarantee consistency in quality at limitless scale at predictably low cost. Whether you outsource to other service providers or freelance contractors, the most you can guarantee is lowering your cost and freeing up some time. While this may be great in the short term, for a company that is looking to exponentially grow, it quickly becomes an unscalable solution.

The misconception around outsourcing is that it is always underscored by the 'specialist' ability of the 'outsourcer' to do a better job than anyone inside the company. Many outsourcing providers will also describe their pricing model as the equivalent of 'ten hours of productive time that you could have spent building your business'. When framed in this way, the efficiency-seeking CEO/CFO is left with an almost 'no brainer' decision to free up time. However, longer-term operators will understand the cultural and intellectual impact of this decision and may ask themselves: 'If we can't do our own book-keeping at this size, how will we ever know how to do it when we're ten times bigger?'

In medical terms, outsourcing is a sort of painkiller vs antibiotic comparison; it might relieve you of some short-term discomfort but at some point you're going to need to address the root of the problem. How and when will you be able to if in the early years you outsourced it? Following the same analogy, just as a painkiller prevents your body from building up its own natural immunity from fighting similar illnesses in future, a culture of whimsically outsourcing seemingly time-consuming and difficult tasks means your organisation never develops a resiliency muscle for problem solving.

Any opportunity to strengthen the 'resiliency muscle' is an exercise that every high-growth company should opt for. There will always be suppliers, companies and specialists that are willing to quote you for a slice of your margin but succumbing to them in an unintentional manner often says more about your problem-solving manner than your ability to prioritise your time.

Some examples of popularly outsourced tasks from the world of finance that really are better managed in-house are book-keeping and payroll. There are perfectly legitimate reasons why, in the short term, these tasks are outsourced, from time saving to the need to be flawlessly accurate. However, both tasks are so intrinsic to the daily operations of the business that finding ways to automate should always be prioritised over simply outsourcing them. Over time, a company often develops the scale and funding to employ specialists in the finance department to bring these sorts of tasks back in-house. But if the leadership of the company is not well versed in these processes, they will be unable to provide any direction to a newly employed finance department, nor will they have in any way evolved those processes in line with the business's needs.

Often, only upon the hiring of an internal finance person, usually after having secured some funding, does the company wake up to the significance of tasks such as accurate book-keeping. While outsourcing is usually the reason behind the delay in this realisation, undertaking an exercise in automating the lion's share of similar tasks can provide a solution that ensures critical knowledge and learning are retained among key personnel without being a burden on time.

Taking this sort of approach to mundane and repetitive tasks not only strengthens the 'resiliency muscle' but also supports the suggestion that outsourcing is often a misdirected automation opportunity. Senior leaders will find that this attitude inevitably compounds and finds its way into other areas of the organisation, leading at the very least to increased efficiency and self-sufficiency.

Summary

- Automation is an efficiency culture; outsourcing is a deflection of your responsibilities at a cost.

- Choosing a platform service upon which to build your reporting framework needs to be a decision that considers the future.

- Never compromise on the minimum requirements the platform needs to have for your business, eg it connects to your bank account.

- Ensure you allow yourself the most flexibility with add-on software based on the kind of functionality you may require down the line.

- Don't ever feel forced to fit your business to the software. It is better to use simple systems that work than elaborate ones that don't.

- Always be automating and never underestimate the real cost of outsourcing.

9
Everyone's Everywhere – Managing A Remote Finance Team

In the evolution of company culture and work-life practices, 2020 will forever been known as the year that disrupted all tradition. The effects of national lockdowns and the need for social distancing meant companies were forced to embrace distributed teams where they may previously have been hesitant. Workplace productivity software provider Slack produced a 'Remote work in the age of Covid-19' report, which estimated that 16 million US knowledge workers had started working remotely due to Covid-19 as of 27 March 2020.[11]

Many firms were faced with the challenge of re-imagining their HR policies but also the culture they

---

11 Slack Report, 'Remote work in the age of Covid-19: insights from Slack', Slack (2020), https://slack.com/intl/en-gb/resources/why-use-slack/remote-work-in-the-age-of-covid-19, accessed 25 June 2021

aspired to achieve, from a distance. Among our clients, particularly small companies, those that found the transition easiest were those that already had a culture of following prescriptive policies for given scenarios. It therefore begs the question: how should the finance function evolve to accommodate the new normal?

To answer, we must first understand which challenges, brought about through remote working, immediately become the responsibility of the finance function to solve. My observations are as follows:

- There is inherently less visibility on metrics around the business. Working remotely creates timing lags between requesting data from finance and receiving it. Dashboards aside, the appreciation for performance indicators felt in a physical office runs the risk of being diluted at a distance.

- Knowledge sharing between the finance function and the wider team becomes strained. The propensity to ask questions is limited by the drag of having to send an email or instant message where a quick conversation may have previously solved it. Learning is therefore stunted.

- New challenges present themselves because of remote working that do not have documented solutions. These could be: what is the company's reimbursement policy for setting up an office at home? How can employee motivation be safeguarded when there is no obvious divide between work and home life? More broadly, does the structure of the team – its roles and responsibilities – need to adapt for remote situations specifically?

None of the measures outlined in this book were written on the assumption the team in question were all sitting within the same office. Implementation of tools and frameworks such as the Finance Bible, dashboard metrics and the automation framework allow a company to make a smooth transition into establishing additional policies for a new working arrangement.

However, the implementation of a remote working framework for small business finance teams is a unique project that must be tackled specifically. Establishing core principles allows for specific details to be unearthed. In small businesses, it is this level of thinking that is often missing and therefore leads to disjointed practices, with no core beliefs to fall back on.

Aims

- Provide extraordinary support to the wider team and each other.

- Ensure there is no compromise on quality and accuracy of routine work.

- Ensure any gaps in knowledge are discussed and subsequent learnings are shared with everybody.

Remote working method and mantra

Over-communicate

For each company, the implementation of this will be different in accordance with the established culture (video calls, Slack channels or phone calls), but every member of the finance team should be looking to over-communicate across the company. If the intention of the outreach is made clear, it is likely to face less resistance: 'As part of the finance team's effort to ensure you are supported, please let me know if there are any issues cropping up in your area that I can help with. Oh, also, would you mind sending me a receipt for that cab ride you claimed for?'

Display trustworthiness and integrity

This is a vow that sounds implicit but needs to be reaffirmed when a team is experiencing discomfort. You must be for your teammates what you want them to be for you. As a starting point, it may be valuable to send teammates ad hoc performance reports when they have performed well. Not only does this reinforce the measurement culture but it helps maintain morale from a distance.

Training and connection

The CFO must arrange regular sessions for the finance function to talk through scenarios and concepts that people struggle with. It is imperative to establish an open culture of discussion in a distributed setting where teammates are not intimidated to speak candidly. Displaying empathy for everybody's development, especially when they are working in isolation, will not only prevent inaccuracies but also make it an enjoyable dynamic.

Housekeeping for remote working

- Make sure technology and security protocols are in line with the level of confidentiality required for your line of work, eg ensure firewalls work.

- Amend employment contracts to adjust for home working environments as well as the expectations of staff.

- Ensure adequate tax and legal advice is taken with regards to the locations of staff members (there are now a number of online payroll companies that handle multi-jurisdictional employment taxes).

- Ensure staff members have a safe environment in which to work.

There is no escaping the fact that distributed teams are here to stay. While a lot of the benefits are obvious, the associated problems take time to reveal themselves. In the absence of being able to read body language and demeanour, the need for virtual policies is even more important. However, there are significant opportunities to embrace cost saving measures such as the reduced need for physical office space. These funds can be directed to more impactful areas such as R&D or the continuing development of staff through training courses and materials.

Summary

- Over-communicating is a concept your team must become familiar with in a remote working environment. Lay the foundations for this early and set an example by caveating 'check-ins' with disarming phrases such as 'I hope you don't mind me confirming again that I have understood your request correctly?'

- Lack of investment in technology will quickly demotivate a team from performing at their best in a distributed setting. There will always be unexpected hiccups but there is now no excuse for failing to ensure your team has the correct equipment. There are now several organisations designed specifically to assist companies with managing remote and distributed teams with matters ranging from cross border payroll to equipment procurement.

- The finance department will quickly be seen as a source of trust for staff across the organisation. It is only through this dynamic that any potential problem areas will be discovered early enough for them to be addressed. Gestures such as providing positive performance reports, as well as rewarding the department that claims their expenses in time, for example, will go a long way.

- Employment contracts must be amended to account for remote working clauses for the protection of both the staff member and the company. It is advisable that lawyers are engaged to ensure a boilerplate set of documents can be used in all circumstances.

- Training must be reinforced in a remote working environment. While it is important that staff stay abreast with technical matters of both a financial and regulatory nature, it is also vital that the company encourages staff to undertake training to manage stress and mental health. One undeniable and irreplaceable benefit of the physical workspace was the ability for colleagues to support each other in unplanned and ad hoc ways. The company must ensure that this kind of support is in some way replaced by a virtual provision for the benefit of its staff.

10
Taxation Tips –
The Low Hanging Fruit

The final nugget that gets lost in the world of confusing accountancy advice is a basic set of tax 'hacks' that all new businesses should be thinking about.

There is nothing remotely sinister in any of the topics I am about to discuss; these are efficiencies that every entrepreneur should at least be made aware of. If you then decide that for your own reasons you don't wish to pursue any of them, so be it. More often than not, the gap between a founder's knowledge and an accountant's ability to simply articulate complex concepts is too wide to even consider discussing these ideas.

That is not only a shame but a huge contributing factor to why some businesses seem to get off to a flying start while others are seemingly always finding their feet in the early years. I have experienced this issue countless times from the perspective of phone calls from entrepreneurs who aren't even clients: 'My friend has done X but my accountant says we can't do that. It didn't fully make sense to me but does that make sense to you?' The phrasing of this question alone is a classic example of the adviser-client paradox at play. The client knows that they need something but they're not sure exactly what and thus ask a question that doesn't adequately frame the problem. All that they do know is that they are fundamentally afraid of being blind-sided by something that they should have known about.

Let's do what we can to demystify some of those concepts, tax by tax.

VAT

I am going to start with the most polarising tax first. On a basic level, most people think of VAT as the following:

- A tax we incur, a lot

- A tax that at some point we are going to have to charge (and therefore will need to adjust our pricing for)

- A tax that has different rates and treatments in different circumstances, with no obvious formula to what is applicable and when

- A tax that gets infinitely more complicated when working online and (worse) across borders

- A tax that since Brexit will be next to impossible to navigate

Just these points alone could form the basis of a stand-alone book on VAT, but let's stick to what is relevant for a new business looking to scale. I will hypothesise that your fundamental drivers are cashflow efficiency and operational accuracy.

Most people understand that businesses that sell taxable supplies in excess of £85,000 (VAT threshold in 2021) are obliged to register for VAT, apply the prevailing VAT rate to their sales and file VAT returns on a period (usually quarterly) basis. The VAT payable or recoverable to or from HMRC is the net of total VAT collected via sales less the total VAT incurred through purchases and expenses.

For early-stage businesses, it is conceivable that far more VAT is being incurred (through payments) than is being collected (through sales) and significant cashflow is lost accordingly. The solution to this problem is to apply for voluntary registration and thus create a situation where each of your VAT returns is a net refund and that incurred cashflow is returned to the company as quickly as possible. This might sound too good to be true or even potentially laden with complexity and administration, but it is not.

Psychologically, we have all been led to believe that VAT-registered businesses only become so after getting to a certain 'large' size. This is a failure of dialogue between advisers and the start-up community, primarily driven by the culture of negative cashflow businesses losing money before their business model is proven, being relatively new to the adviser world. What is the commitment you make for this privilege? Nothing you aren't already doing if you are at this point in the book. You will need to file a VAT return to HMRC that is not only mathematically accurate (software will handle that) but also supported with invoices and receipts for each transaction (software will handle that too). You must undertake to HMRC that you intend on making taxable supplies in the future; you should ensure you are reclaiming any VAT incurred leading up to that point.

Businesses should also consider changing their VAT filing frequency to monthly rather than the more usual quarterly. This will hasten the frequency with which 'locked' cashflow is paid back to the company. Remember, 'cash is king'.

VAT FILING EXAMPLE

Quarterly

1 January: supplier payment made: £1,000 + VAT = £1,200

VAT quarters: March, June, September, December

VAT quarter 31 March:
- total output VAT: £0
- total input VAT: £200
- total repayable: £200

VAT quarter 31 March due for submission by 7 May
£200 credited in account by (roughly) 15 May

Expense incurred → refund received = 4.5 months

Monthly

1 January: supplier payment made: £1,000 + VAT = £1,200

VAT months: every month

VAT month 31 January:
- total output VAT: £0
- total input VAT: £200
- total repayable: £200

VAT quarter 31 January due for submission by 7 March
£200 credited in account by (roughly) 15 March

Expense incurred → refund received = 2.5 months

This is a significant reduction in the time it takes for a business to access repayment of VAT and thus prevents there being any funding gaps in working capital. HMRC are aware of this and give the business multiple opportunities to apply for monthly filing over quarterly: at the point of registration or at any point in the future when a company may decide that more frequent filings would be an efficient decision.

As with anything, there is a flip side – a commitment on the part of the company to make twelve filings where it would have ordinarily made four. It is maybe for this reason that the decision to switch to monthly filings is met with some trepidation, as it gives 'eight more occasions for you to potentially get something wrong' (a comment relayed to me by a founder from his accountants). If you have learned anything from this book, it should be that with a heavy reliance on well-designed processes and easy to use software, scale and accuracy cease to be a threat to modern-day businesses. It won't matter how many returns you are required to file, as the software will be able to produce them with one click.

Corporation tax

Corporation tax is paid on your profits and payable nine months and one day after the financial year end. The only efficiencies a new business can look to implement relate to ensuring the liability is as efficient as it reasonably can be.

For example, companies deduct expenses to arrive at profit but claim 'capital allowances' for purchases of assets that are bought for the exclusive benefit of the business, eg computer equipment and machinery. Simple decisions such as purchasing your assets before the closing of the financial year versus a few days afterwards can save the company from declaring a higher taxable profit figure than necessary for a given period. As a result, the tax payable could easily be reduced or completely avoided. Tips like this might sound almost too simplistic to even warrant a mention but the days up to and including the end of the financial year often pass finance teams by, only for them to later realise that some attention could have resulted in real savings.

However, for many early-stage businesses, having expenditure regularly outweigh revenue means that they are often in a loss-making position for tax purposes. Losses accumulate on a year-by-year basis and are then rolled forward to be offset against future profits.

Many of these expenses may well have been incurred by the founders/directors on a personal basis. The line between a hobby, side project and full-fledged business can become blurred when a team is small and hopes are high. One invaluable tip for this period of time is to maintain a record of all expenses incurred by the directors for crediting to what is known as a 'director's loan account'. This is no different to you or your fellow co-founders having lent money to the business and keeping a record of how much is owed back. The importance of maintaining this record is three-fold; first, as the expenses incurred were really for the company to pay, those deductions need to be included in the company's P&L account. Second, as the business did not make those payments from its own resources, it needs to recognise on its balance sheet that it owes that money back to the director. Third, as the director is owed that sum of money, they are at liberty to withdraw those funds as a repayment of loan at any point of their choosing, without it being misconstrued as taxable income.

HMRC will expect directors to be able to produce documentary evidence up to six years after the tax year to which it applies. As a result, to access the benefits to the director and company as well as comply with statutory requirements, it is advisable that the director maintains a personal expenses sheet (a template can be found at www.thefinancedepartment.co). This can be provided to the finance team or accountants on a periodic basis to ensure transactions that are taking place outside the business bank account are also being captured within the financials.

Research and development tax credits

One effective way of utilising these losses is through pursuing R&D tax credits. While R&D tax credits are not limited to loss-making businesses only, the chance to trade those rolled forward losses for a cash credit of up to 33% of your R&D expenditure is an unavoidable opportunity. Why would you wait to use those losses against tax bills in the future when you can trade them for cash now?

There are a couple of misconceptions about R&D tax credits; the first is that they are only available to ultra-high-tech businesses (think lab coats and Bunsen burners). This is false – any business that can claim to have made an advancement in science and technology may apply.

What does that mean? Any technical project or innovation that had an uncertain outcome before you embarked on it would qualify. Unsurprisingly, given the definition, it has largely been technology companies that have realised R&D tax credits apply to them, though a proper understanding of the legislation has meant successful applications for drinks companies, fashion brands, manufacturing plants, construction companies and even a (famous) biscuit company!

It is not only advisable to consider any opportunities to claim for R&D tax credits but you should also prepare your finances on an ongoing basis to align with the submission format HMRC require. HMRC will always want to understand what the specific innovation projects are and what the costs directly incurred to administer the project were. Software can be customised to create a tagging capability against transactions so that at the end of the financial year, a report showing the R&D qualifying expenditure is simple to generate. Equipping the business with these capabilities means that not only can additional (and often critical) cashflow be accessed quickly and efficiently, but the business can also proactively engage in this conversation with advisers who will always end up charging more if such systems are not in place.

The reframing of tax efficiencies as being in the hands of the company rather than advisers can be achieved as a by-product of processes and automation. The results on a basic level are increased capital efficiency and accuracy. More importantly, the benefits of proactive financial management run deep into the core and culture of the organisation, which then compounds across the disciplines. Generating that extra headspace, clarity, control and productivity not only has a tangible impact on morale, but it also assists with taking away pressure that can build to become crippling for senior management. All the above suggestions have cash benefits that ultimately extend runway and reduce reliance on external investors.

With access to more of this kind of information, founders are at liberty to tackle tax efficiencies without the looming fear of HMRC that has so successfully blunted this capability to date. The fear of being investigated is directly correlated with the founder's lack of knowledge and confidence in tax concepts and internal processes. I urge you to leave that fear behind and commit to a new era of the empowered founder.

Summary

- Companies should quickly get to grips with how filing monthly VAT returns may be the answer to short-term funding gaps.

- Don't miss out on cashflow efficiencies for the perceived extra 'work' or compliance.

- Compliance should be a positive by-product of your systems, not the other way around

- Always ensure the finance function has a dialogue at least three months before the financial year end to discuss strategies to maximise corporation tax efficiencies.

- Ensure the directors are maintaining a record of the expenditure and that it is being entered into the company financials on a regular basis.

- R&D tax credits are available for any company that can display an advancement in science and technology. Do not take this too literally – it can apply in many related situations. Speak to an expert as early as possible and ensure that financials are set up in a way to limit the amount of work required to prepare a claim.

- Being tax efficient is a discipline that can underpin your resilient fortress. This goal alone forces process discipline, clarity of thought and accuracy in data. Don't run before you can walk but learn to walk quickly.

11

Effective Fundraising – The Minimal Viable Processes

A common feature of high-growth enterprises is the need for external capital to maintain and accelerate momentum over an inorganic period. There are many reasons why it is necessary for a company on the cutting edge of industry to manage capital requirements this way. Examples of this include:

- The costs of starting that are too high to 'bootstrap' the initial expenses

- Needing to quickly get a head start in an emergent industry to be known as a market leader

- Capitalising on a specific opportunity that is only available in a limited window of time

- Entering an industry where it is quantifiably punitive to have limited resources, eg a luxury retailer

The funding landscape is varied, with all the options broadly broken down between debt and equity. For the purposes of this chapter, we will focus on equity capital as it is often the option that requires the most thought when considering the process. It is also the most common form of finance for early-stage businesses. We will talk later about the stakeholders involved and what their motivations are, but it stands to reason that equity capital is initially sought from friends and family and latterly from institutional investors such as venture capitalists and family offices.

The dialogue around asking an investor to part with their money is mostly conjecture articulated by the management of the investment-seeking start-up. Almost all the profit-making opportunity being presented will be forward looking via a business plan. To support these plans, investment decks are then padded out with markers to support the assumptions the founders have made. The credentials of the team are used to reassure potential investors that their money is in the safe hands of professionals with a track record in doing 'important' things.

General fundraising

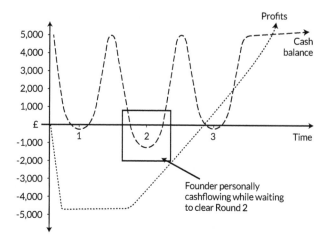

Fundraising rounds

Obtaining an understanding of different capital instruments is important before embarking on dialogue with potential suitors. When is debt better than equity? What does £100k from Investor A mean vs £200k from Investor B? When can a convertible loan be appropriate? These are all worthwhile riddles that have different answers for different companies. However, before indulging in these questions, it is important to look 'under the hood' of the company to understand whether the fundamental housekeeping and processes have been organised in an investible way. Where you are today says a lot about where you're going. If you can't efficiently manage a small enterprise, it is unlikely to fill an investor with much confidence about your growth prospects and there are only so many deficiencies that you can pin to being 'under-resourced'. Many of these lessons are discussed in detail throughout this book but there is an etiquette to fundraising readiness that warrants special focus.

General process: one-off

Build a cashflow model as soon as possible and understand your funding requirements over a meaningful time horizon, ie twelve to twenty-four months. Do not be led to believe that a timeframe beyond this holds any value as it simply does not, at least at this stage. With a reliable one- to two-year horizon you can prioritise expenditure as well as investor relations. Update this model every month.

SEIS and EIS

Investors in the UK are becoming increasingly familiar with the Seed Enterprise Investment Scheme and Enterprise Investment Scheme (SEIS/EIS), which were introduced by the government to incentivise high-net worth individuals to invest equity capital into early-stage businesses through tax rebates. This has proven to be an excellent catalyst for investment, with many businesses accessing pools of capital that may not have been previously available.

It is astounding how many founders do not optimise their businesses to be SEIS/EIS-ready. The HMRC website is not easy to follow at the best of times and, as a result, critical details around time limits, employment restrictions, eligible and ineligible investors get missed and cause trouble when it is sometimes too late to rectify.

Below is a list of common mistakes and pitfalls for entrepreneurs:

- You cannot buy a business and then use one of the schemes to raise capital for growth – it must be organically developed.

- You cannot benefit from SEIS or EIS as a founder or shareholder who has (at any point) owned more than 30% of the share capital.

- Your (direct) family members cannot benefit from SEIS or EIS – routing your funds through them is not an option.

- Employees cannot benefit from either scheme.

- Companies become ineligible for SEIS two years after trade began. Trade does not equal incorporation date; it means trading, ie buying and selling products or services.

- SEIS and EIS shares cannot benefit from any special rights or attributes other than those available to any other common shareholder.

- Seeking advanced assurance is not mandatory but is advisable. Remember, it is not a certificate, you are still at risk of breaching the SEIS/EIS rules if you do not continue to adhere to the rules throughout the life of the company.

If you believe that SEIS/EIS investors are going to be important sources of capital for your business, it is important to undertake an assessment as early as possible to ensure there are no limiting factors to your plans. Once you are ready to embark upon your fundraising journey, it becomes compelling to be able to say that the investment is SEIS/EIS eligible. However, not every business will be eligible to apply and HMRC have an explicit list of restricted industries and trades on their website. If all the above is in order, they will be open to an application for 'advanced assurance', to which they will provide an approval, which can then be used as a comfort note to show investors.

Once a round of funding has been secured, it is incumbent upon the company to complete the necessary paperwork with HMRC to not only notify them of the round but also self-certify compliance and authority to receive and distribute SEIS/EIS certificates to eligible investors. Issuing the shares for the same funding round on the same date prevents multiple submissions, as they will tend to consider each date a separate event.

Your investors' ongoing ability to benefit from that tax relief is the responsibility of the company to remain compliant throughout the life of their investment.

SEIS/EIS process: one-off

Ask your accountant or lawyer to perform an SEIS suitability review for your plans to ensure there is nothing within the legislation you may have missed. It is catastrophic to identify these issues once investors have been introduced into the business, and frankly irresponsible. To ensure you are undertaking this process efficiently, you should provide the following information: the nature of your business, a summary of your strategic plans, an indication of your funding requirements over one to two years and who you believe will be your investors.

Companies House

One of the fundamental tenets of good governance is to ensure that the company legal documentation is not only accurate but also accurately reflected at Companies House. This is a public register where anyone can search the names of the directors, the company registered address, published accounts and other pertinent secretarial notifications.

The register held online is supposed to be an online representation of what are known as the company

THE FINANCE PLAYBOOK FOR ENTREPRENEURS

statutory books. As a minimum, statutory books comprise:

- Register of members (shareholders)
- Register of directors
- Persons of significant control

It is the directors' statutory obligation to ensure that any changes to the above registers are not only reflected within the company's records but subsequently also updated on Companies House. Anyone can request to view a copy of the statutory registers and they must be available to inspect either at the company's registered office or at another address that company officials have nominated.

Ordinarily, entrepreneurs rarely pay much attention to the completeness of these records until, within a moment's notice, an investor's lawyer asks to inspect them. While this may feel like a low priority administrative task, the number of examples I could provide of companies that have had to pay thousands in legal fees to retrospectively fix their registers is eye-watering. That's without getting into the resultant reputational damage in front of the new investor who may have only recently committed to the investment.

Getting the small things right is a strategy that always pays dividends.

'Cap table' management

One of the basic statutory records a company must maintain is known as a register of members or capitalisation (cap) table. This is a dynamic document that highlights the entire audit trail of shareholders. In a fast-growing enterprise, this document can quickly escalate with new names, details and figures that become difficult to stay on top of.

While the statutory obligation is important, it is vital that management maintain a fully functional version of this document for their own records, particularly when multiple investors are introduced via multiple funding rounds. Beyond being a record, it is also the document through which management base their calculations of future funding rounds, valuations and dilution.

When thinking about relevant information, ask yourself whether you can instantly answer the following questions simply by glancing at your cap table:

- How many shareholders does the company have?

- What price per share did each shareholder pay?

- Which investors were covered by the SEIS/EIS scheme?

- What is the total share capital of the business?

- What was the share capital of the business after each funding round?

- What was the share capital of the business at each financial year end?

- How many classes of shares is the equity split into?

- What is the nominal price of each share class?

- What date were the shares issued to each shareholder?

- What is the full address of each shareholder?

There are many online tools available to assist with this but typically companies will maintain a spreadsheet too (a template is available at www.thefinancedepartment.co). As a company grows, your investment in such processes and systems will become increasingly more rewarding. The business may introduce an employee share option scheme or want to simulate scenarios of potential future investors, all of which are impossible to calculate without a well-functioning cap table.

Company secretarial process: quarterly

Check the company registers and cap table are up to date for any changes in details such as directors, shareholders, addresses or persons of significant control. These need to be reconciled against the filings at Companies House to ensure they are accurately reflected. This process will save a lot of hassle later.

Other tips

1. Create a new share class for every major funding round – this not only makes it easier to identify different shareholders, but it also provides a chronology to the classes that allows current and prospective investors to keep track of their investment. Further, it presents the equity of the company in a way that allows for a clear separation between different categories of shareholder, eg founders, SEIS investors, EIS investors, regular investors, venture capitalists and employees.

2. Ensure you have a financial model that logically works back to the valuation you have raised at each funding round. It is important for the company to always be able to track back to the growth metrics that influenced share price, so that future issuances can be marked up (or down) accordingly. Not only will this present the future of your business in an 'investible' way, it also gives the wider company a blueprint upon which to operate.

3. Always implement any employee share options plans (eg EMI scheme) as early as possible. Other than ensuring your staff are motivated with a

long-term incentive plan, from a fundraising perspective, investors will always want an understanding of what their shareholding is likely to be diluted (reduced) by via an inevitable equity compensation scheme.

4. Use a segregated bank account to collect investor money – while this is not a legal requirement, the ability to segregate your investor funds makes things administratively simpler from a book-keeping perspective as well as a legal due diligence standpoint.

5. Ensure a well-ordered numbering system for share certificates is maintained so that an audit trail of which shareholders hold which shares is easily understandable.

6. Use an electronic signature service to ensure your documentation is not only automated but also paperless. This will reduce the time it takes to process the reams of paper involved while also preventing documents going missing.

Summary

- Companies that are unable to grow through their own resources will likely consider raising equity capital through the early stages of their existence.

- To ensure the company's priorities are adequately planned, it is imperative that the company builds a cashflow forecast model that tracks the funding requirements over a reliable time frame, eg twelve to twenty-four months.

- To maximise efficiency in the fundraising process, it is advisable for the company to follow an easy-to-implement set of processes as a matter of routine to avoid retrospective problems.

- Tax-advantaged fundraising options are always an attractive source of equity capital in certain situations. Companies wishing to make use of these schemes should be familiar with their requirements, pitfalls and disqualifying criteria well ahead of any proposed fundraising round.

- Seeking small efficiencies in early fundraising processes will provide amplified benefits as the company grows and considers larger rounds of funding.

- Due diligence is lowering the drawbridge to the fortress and inviting guests in to come and make their own judgements on the fruits of your hard work.

Conclusion

The topics and suggestions in this book have been carefully curated over many years of conversations with early-stage businesses, distilling the common problems and presenting them as a single source of wisdom. This is an important distinction to make, as these lessons have been tested across hundreds of companies as opposed to being the musings of one single adviser. It is for this reason that this book can serve as a complete foundation for any professional or start-up looking to rapidly grow.

Over the last twenty years we have lived through unprecedented advances in technology, business models, practices and outcomes. The velocity of change meant many advisers were themselves in new territory, with old methods and ways of thinking rendered tired and obsolete. Understanding the impact of e-commerce and a flood of new cloud-based softwares that disrupted long-embedded incumbents left many advisers wrong footed. Simultaneously, for the first time in history the generational gap between clients and their advisers widened to the point where genuine familiarity and empathy became difficult to extend.

Early-stage businesses were therefore left with a fragmented knowledge base and network with no single source of truth or structure coming to the fore. There is no fundamental source of truth for the business of today. Two seemingly identical businesses may require completely different advice, advisers and skill sets but neither the adviser world nor the entrepreneurial world were equipped to recognise that. In that environment, this book makes the case to empower your foundations and processes internally and only seek externally what is genuinely valuable. The concept of the fortress comes from the theme that companies must strive to be self-sufficient, robust and impenetrable to face the challenges of modern enterprise.

Whether you are a new founder or an incoming CFO for a fast-growing business, it is never too late to re-evaluate the systems upon which the company is being built and take a blunt decision about whether it serves the purpose of the company's existence.

In modern-day businesses, the ability to manage and operate a well-designed set of processes is more valuable than possessing the deep technical knowledge behind them. It is more scalable and directly increases the value per hour worked for everyone in the organisation. This is happening across the board.

The shift has already started; we are moving towards an era of entrepreneur-led intelligence; basic compliance, processes and outcomes are the product of well-designed internal infrastructure and the relationship with select advisers becomes proactive, strategic and technical. To stay ahead of the curve, founders will need to level up in their practical understanding of running a business beyond the lectures of an MBA programme. For CEOs and finance professionals, this book contains the equivalent of multiple conversations with a firm of accountants and lawyers or, at the very least, equips them with the right questions. It is advisable to use both the overarching and the specific lessons mentioned in this book as conversation starters with advisers. With luck this will be the start of a relationship reframing that will bear fruit into the future.

If the last twenty years have taught us anything it is that the highest virtues entrepreneurs and businesses can aspire to are 'adaptability' and 'resilience'. One requirement that will never change is having a structure that serves the fundamental critical success factors of the business and allows you to remain adaptable and resilient. Recognising this fact is step one of the growing up process discussed in an earlier chapter. My colleagues and I have certainly shifted our focus to providing foundational consultancy to finance departments so they can become self-sufficient and self-servicing as early as possible.

Alongside this work we have set up www.thefinancedepartment.co to serve as a repository of tools and materials for this community. Here you will find templates, explanations and knowledge to assist with the challenges facing fast-growing finance departments. We aim to continue to fill the gap between advisers and entrepreneurs and equip you with easy-to-digest information, updates and explanations on topics that will enable you to ask the right questions of your advisers.

Acknowledgements

This book is dedicated to many people, but most of all to my family, who have each taught and inspired me in unquantifiable ways. I am thankful beyond words.

My father, Naim, whose untimely passing put me on this journey; wherever you are, I hope you can see your name in print, Dad. My mother, who gave her all to ensure we were able to explore every opportunity that life threw at us; an outlook that led two young Asian boys from North-West London to believe that one of them could one day write a book and the other become a roaring success at whatever he puts his mind to (I'm the former, in case it wasn't obvious). I thank my younger brother, Omair, whose example, encouragement and support fuels me with pride and ambition in equal measure.

To my inspirational wife, Najah, who like many others in the National Health Service spent almost all of 2020 away from her family treating the dreaded virus. The days and nights she spent at the hospital gave me the time to start this book, but trying to keep up with her work ethic is what got me to the end. To my children, Anayah and Nyel, you are both my world.

The Author

Having started in business from a young age and trained as a chartered accountant, Asif now wears many hats.

His primary role is to serve as an adviser to multiple high-growth entrepreneurs and businesses, often venture backed, on matters ranging from accounting and taxation to growth and strategy. This experience afforded him the opportunity to also advise the UK Government on matters affecting the entrepreneurial community, particularly with reference to changes to the tax system, as well as the ongoing effort to make the United Kingdom an effective and enterprising ecosystem.

More recently, Asif has focused on his belief that *access* to good quality, reliable information is crucial to the evolution and maturity of entrepreneurs, none less than matters pertaining to finance and specifically finance departments. This book is the first codification of that knowledge with an ever-evolving platform available at www.thefinancedepartment.co

Beyond work, Asif is a family man, sportsman and actively involved in charity work with multiple organisations specifically dedicated to hunger alleviation.

🌐 Asifahmed.co

in www.linkedin.com/in/asifahmed2/

🐦 a_ahmed